Pra

Unmasking

Taken captive by subtle lies, held prisoner by invisible bonds, silenced by shame...now is the time for the manipulative games to stop! Form your plan of escape.

"Meredith Wesley offers bare-knuckle strategies to help anyone targeted by a manipulator get a clear grasp of their situation and identify practical ways to shift from oppression to agency and, ultimately, freedom."

—Manya Wakefield
Recovery Coach and Founder, Narcissistic Abuse Rehab, Author, *Are You In An Emotionally Abusive Relationship?*

"Meredith uncovers the manipulator's tactics with clarity and simplicity. *Unmasking Manipulation* is a must read for victims of emotional and psychological abuse. This quick read will help victims see through the fog and begin to rebuild their lives."

—Anne Blythe, MEd
Betrayal Trauma Recovery Podcast, Founder of btr.org, Author, *Trauma Mama Husband Drama*

"Unmasking manipulation approaches the subject of coercive control with elegance, sensitivity, and intellect. Those suffering in a confusing and frightening relationship will benefit enormously from the insight offered and will carefully move out of the darkness into the light. A captivating read!"

—Rachel Watson
Author, *How To Annihilate A Narcissist In the Family Courts*

"To awaken from the dream that is manipulation is to come face-to-face with a troubling reality. There are those who wear masks and pretend to be your friend when in fact they are your foe. For victims of manipulation to heal, they must first recognize that their ability to make independent choices has been hijacked through cleverly disguised mind games by a self-serving manipulator. Meredith offers victims of manipulation the opportunity to clearly understand this form of abuse . . . as they navigate the healing journey ahead. Reclaiming the mind takes time, and Meredith's knowledge of this subject matter is sure to be a comfort for anyone looking to free themselves from the grips of psychological manipulation."

—Lisa A. Romano
Life Coach and Bestselling Author, *The Codependency Manifesto: Clearing the Way Out of the Codependent Mind*

.

"Meredith Wesley's book is a must read for anyone who has or has had the challenge of disengaging from a Manipulator. She has excellent examples, distinctions, and strategies by which to identify and free yourself from the Manipulator. However, my assessment, the true value of this book is her choice of words . . . [:] You are going to battle. You need to understand the Manipulator is an enemy not an ally. You need a war strategy. You need to understand the dangers of not engaging in the fight. Many people choose to become 'nicer' during times of stress. She is very clear on why that strategy won't work. She leads you skillfully into becoming a formidable opponent to the Manipulator. Meredith Wesley's words must become your guiding light: 'Evil will freely prevail until you engage it in battle. It needs to feel the force of justice.'"

—Dr. Anne Brown RNCS
Author, *Backbone Power the Science of Saying No*

Anita
07719 001433

Unmasking Manipulation

Maneuvering the Undertow with
Shrewdness and Innocence

By Meredith Wesley

© Copyright 2020 Meredith Wesley

ISBN 978-1-64663-243-5

Published by

 köehlerbooks™

3705 Shore Drive
Virginia Beach, VA 23455
800–435–4811
www.koehlerbooks.com

UNMASKING MANIPULATION

*Maneuvering the Undertow with
Shrewdness and Innocence*

MEREDITH WESLEY

VIRGINIA BEACH
CAPE CHARLES

To the unsung martyrs
who die a little bit every day
to uphold a flicker of hope
in their dark world

*"Freedom is never voluntarily given by the oppressor;
it must be demanded by the oppressed."*

—Martin Luther King, Jr.

THE CONTENT OF THIS MANUAL is written in the second person. This is not to suggest that you have personally experienced what is being described or that you necessarily relate at all, but it is more for the clarity of discussion. So I apologize now for anything that is offensive, foreign, or inconceivable to you. It is not at all that I expect you to be as I describe, but if at points you are, then I want you to know that you are understood. Even if you are not there personally just now, perhaps too the voice will lend empathy to those who are. Anyone who is entangled in manipulation certainly needs a bit of genuine concern.

The manipulator is largely referred to as masculine. This is not to suggest that they cannot be feminine. However, because of historical and social forces, rightly or wrongly, the majority are men. Please replace pronouns as necessary.

Here overall, the extreme case is described, where it totters just under the bar of outright cruelty. In all earnestness, I hope that your case is not so severe. But if it becomes so, there is still hope.

Table of Contents

12
MOVING FORWARD

1
THE MANIPULATION GAME

CHASE AND LESLIE have just moved to a new city for Chase's new job. He started working very shortly after the move, and now Leslie is in charge of getting the house settled. Their two boys, ages six and nine, begin classes at their new school. Meanwhile, Leslie continues to struggle with a physical issue that her old doctors could not identify before the move. Today is her first appointment with the new physician, and she is grateful that they exerted the effort to schedule her visit without the usual six-week delay. Unfortunately, the appointment clashes with the boys' schedule, who leave school at the same time. As the solution, Chase has agreed to come home early to meet the bus.

Anxious to get on good terms with his bosses, Chase speaks with the company's president and offers him an invitation to dinner that evening. The president, Mr. Harden, suspects that his employee's wife might object, but Chase quickly assures him that because Leslie is so lonely since the move, she would be delighted to host company. Mr. Harden presses Chase to call and make sure, so Chase dials right there and puts her on speaker.

"Hey, honey, you'd never guess. I've been talking with the president here. We got to talking about what an amazing cook you are, and he wants to come over for dinner. You don't mind, do you?"

Leslie is polite. "No, he is very welcome."

"Good. What time is good for you, Mr. Harden?"

"We usually dine at six thirty, but I do not want to trouble you."

"No trouble at all! Six thirty will give you a whole extra hour to prepare something extra special, Les. You're a doll. Bye."

Leslie's mind swarms with potential protests, but Chase hung up before she could graciously object. She reflects then calls Chase's personal line several times before getting through. Chase cheerfully proclaims that Mr. Harden is looking forward to dinner and expounds on how much of a benefit this will be for his job security, even suggesting elaborate dishes that she could make.

Finally, Leslie voices her concerns: her doctor's appointment, the house upheaval, and her poor health. Chase lightly counters them all: "Reschedule the appointment. They haven't found anything wrong with you anyway," "Your everyday meals are good enough for the Hardens," "They won't mind a few boxes," and "After all, you promised. I can't go and tell him you've changed your mind."

Leslie focuses on the most urgent issue. She says that she can't very well reschedule the appointment. Chase retorts, "You can. You just don't want to."

"Then I need you to help with the dinner when you come home early for the boys."

"Oh, about that: I can't make it home before six tonight. Besides, traffic would make it too impossible."

"Then what am I supposed to do?"

"Go make friends with the neighbors. I'm sure you'll find someone willing to babysit."

"What?!"

"You're smart. You can figure it out. Look, I've got to go. Bye."

Leslie is left waiting for school to get out, arriving late at the doctor's office with two boys and their complaints in tow, rushing to make some meal partially worthy of the built-up expectations, and enduring the shame of a messy house and inexplicable health limitations. Through it all, she must be perfectly pleasant and attentive to her guests.

Thoroughly embarrassed by the whole affair, she addresses it with Chase that night. He answers, "What's the matter? So you've made a bad call, and you had to deal with it. I didn't have any problem with it. What does it matter anyway? It all worked out."

Leslie tries to explain but is abruptly cut off with, "I'm not going to discuss it anymore. I'm beat." She knows better than to bother bringing it up again.

This exchange is more than an absentminded husband whose career priorities trump his wife's personal concerns. It is manipulation.

Manipulation wants to make the unnatural appear natural. It wants illusions to appear real; fantasies to be a reality; deceptions to seem truer than truth. Manipulation looks to redefine normal. It wants what is harmful to appear helpful; what is wrong to appear right; what is unjust to appear just. It calls futility success and curses blessings. It has learned to define the emotional climate of most situations to sway feeling toward its own purpose. It hides its sneak attacks behind diplomacy and charm. And it has found its methods satisfyingly effective. But it must do this all with as much stealth as possible. Manipulation works best when the victims remain unaware. They must feel compelled to act without recognizing their freedom of choice is being overridden. The victims' ignorance and confusion are golden and are nurtured with the greatest of care.

Manipulation is all about getting you to do something that you would not naturally do. But it is necessary for it to look natural, as if you have chosen to do it out of sincere desire and deep belief.

Before we act, we think—so it all begins in the mind. Somehow, the manipulator must penetrate your thinking, swaying it towards his own agenda, so that he can get you to "choose" what it is he wants you to do. It is a mind game on its deepest level, and unfortunately, the only way to beat a mind game is to play it. The fairer and more forthright you are, the more ammunition the manipulator has to hurt you in your most vulnerable places—whether you realize what it is he is doing or not. Frankly, it is war. And the manipulator has the advantage because he is the only one who knows it, at first. He is out to get what he wants, regardless of you, and in many cases, with your complete cooperation.

He is an expert deceiver and a master of human nature, especially over those who live by strong principles. He understands what it is you will do and what you will not do, so he pushes you as far as he can to the line he knows you will not cross. All the while, he is adeptly convincing you and others that his behavior is perfectly legitimate. There is a wide variety of tricks he will apply to justify his own behavior and then often turns the argument inside out later to talk you into acting for his advantage. He is unbothered by the inconsistency because that is not his goal. The goal is to get you to serve his agenda. But it always must *seem* right if he is going to get you to swallow it. Whatever it takes to get this to be, he will likely do.

The Healthy Relationship Standard

Finding yourself in a relationship with a manipulator can be very disorienting. Truth is mixed with lies, bad is disguised as good, motivations are hidden, and unspoken boundaries are freely crossed. No investment is made into the hopes and dreams that fueled your relationship at the beginning. The warm feelings are overshadowed by guilt, fear, and shame. Respect has faded. Promises, though still bright, are easily forgotten. Words, though still sweet, never become a reality. The result may look harmonious from the outside, but it feels like utter chaos.

Facing this chaos is a puzzle. Relationships can be complex, and causes and effects can be unclear. Likely there were faults on both sides. Misunderstandings, miscommunication, mistakes all can contribute to the mess. Human weakness and imperfect efforts can add to the disharmony. External problems, people, and strains invariably seep in, too. There are emotional, financial, social, moral, physical, and mental considerations to factor in. It is complicated, and it is difficult to know where to begin to sort it all out.

It is helpful then to return to the basics. Try to step back and honestly evaluate the health of your relationship. Without too much thought or justification, how strong is it (in general) based on the following eight characteristics?

Principles of Healthy Relationships
Mutual trust
- Can you rely on this person to follow through with their promises?
- Will they readily cover your back?
- Do they keep your confidences?
- Do they make good choices?

Mutual respect
- Does this person ask for your opinions—and hear them?
- Do they keep your best interests as a high priority?
- Is there a marked thoughtfulness about them?
- Do you both have a voice?
- Does one personality dominate over the other?

Honesty
- Is truth highly valued by this person, even when it is uncomfortable or unwanted?
- Do they have the courage to face reality as it is?
- Are they willing to look into themselves to see what is ugly there?

Shared responsibility

- Is there a strict division of labor?
- Is there a willingness to take on new roles/jobs to keep things running smoothly?
- When glory or shame come, are both equally shared?
- Are the "house rules" and policies mutually discussed before they are established?

Good communication

- Is there good effort to be clear and to promote mutual understanding?
- Is there communication on multiple levels?
- Is there a willingness to listen and understand?
- Are there topics that are taboo?
- Is there an openness to hearing and expressing emotions?

Individuality

- Are both of you free to develop new interests, a new job direction, and new friendships?
- Can you manage your time, money, and priorities without harsh judgment or pressure?
- Do you have personal goals beyond the relationship and basic responsibilities?

Mutual support

- Do they show genuine interest in your ideas, opinions, passions, and activities?
- Do they sacrifice their own time and priorities to be present at key moments (planned or unplanned)?
- Do they recognize your weaknesses, not to shame you, but to fill in the gaps with their own strength?

Fair fighting

- Is there a mutual respect for reason?
- Is there a respect for due process and justice?
- Do they resort to hurting or betraying others to win a point?

- Is there a willingness to consider new evidence and reevaluate their judgment?
- Is there an acknowledgment of your perspective?
- Do negotiations end in a fair compromise?

Healthy relationships require mature choices by both parties. There needs to be clear and decisive effort in all of these areas by each of you. The ones that are lacking need to be honestly faced and addressed, not dismissed. And these efforts need to be continuous. Respect, honesty, or fairness do not have an expiration date. Maintaining a relationship requires a commitment to these principles all the time. It is mutual effort for mutual benefit.

Once manipulation is regularly applied by one of the parties, however, it all comes crashing down. There is no possibility of a healthy relationship. A healthy person is looking for a partnership for the greater good of both. A manipulator is looking for control only for self-benefit. The goals are opposed and irreconcilable. Holding onto such a relationship leaves his interests far more represented than yours. You become overshadowed by the imbalance, and no amount of working toward holding up your end of the principles will make up for his lack. The relationship is doomed unless different principles are applied.

So if you see that violations of these values are many and frequent on one side while far and few between on the other, the relationship is most certainly unhealthy. If there is great effort to convince you (and others) that it is healthy despite your observations, it is not only unhealthy, it is also manipulative. The true test is what others would observe and think if they saw what was going on behind closed doors. If your life were a movie, how many protagonists would there be?

Now What?
So what if you find that your relationship is unhealthy? Maybe it is even manipulative; now what? The advice is invariably to get out

of it—and do so, if you can! But what if you can't? Maybe you are related and you cannot change your bloodline; maybe it is a work relationship and you cannot afford to quit; maybe it is a marriage and the risk of loss is too huge to consider. This is when people give you a pat on the back, tell you to hang in there, and walk away.

The good news is that there is hope. The bad news is that it is a journey. But the first leg of the journey is one of the mind, which you may take without action, resources, or commitment. If you are trapped in manipulation, then you need to develop a new pattern of thinking for dealing with it. The sensible, open-hearted methods that you might use with people of goodwill will not work. Those warm, inspirational philosophies posted on school walls will lead you astray. It is not a matter of seeking terms of peace but of accepting the acts of aggression as a declaration of war. Only it is psychological warfare. And unless you have been there before, you need training.

Ally or Enemy?

With all of the confusion, it may be difficult to accept that there is a serious hostility. The manipulation can be charming, dynamic, intelligent, or pathetic—not the typical signs of an attack. He can draw us in with his strong personality or emotions. It might not seem like he is doing anything unethical. Because he has moved us to follow him without threat or anger, it looks like it was our choice to move. But that is exactly what illusions are meant to do: draw us in to conclude something that is not right or good. His behavior is not fact but facade. It is a performance.

But how can you be sure? Motivation is everything. Why someone does what he does matters more than almost anything else. It helps us distinguish between whom we can trust and whom we ought to distrust. With deceit, things are often different than what they appear, and it requires a little more digging to reveal the truth. So get ready to dig when weighing his motivation. What he does might be presented as good, but is it really? Did he have good intentions? Unfortunately, we cannot see why others do what they do, so we need to judge them by the next best thing: the end results.

If a friend suddenly pushes you, it is likely to keep you from getting run over. If an enemy pushes you, it is likely to get you run over. The actions are the same, the claims for their reasons may even be the same, but the results are *very* different. How we ought to respond to a push then depends on who is doing the pushing. Is he an ally or an enemy? With manipulation, though, the pushing is done on a psychological level. You are only emotionally run over. There is no physical proof—no blood or ambulance, no dents or skid marks, no police investigation or charges. You are really the only one who can judge the effects of the pushing. And you had best take heed, so you know if you are dealing with an ally or enemy. Though this is far easier to judge with physical evidence, the same principles can be used to judge emotional attacks.

Allies are people who are fighting beside you for the same cause. They have your back; they are interested in keeping you strong. What is to one's advantage is to the other's advantage; it is a partnership. Allies are made not by position, title, or rhetoric, but by faithful action. Your best interest is consistently taken into consideration. They respect your differences. They are eager to contribute their own resources to the cause as well. There is a willingness to work together because the purpose is higher than you both. Cooperation requires some give and take on all sides, but overall, there is mutual agreement for mutual benefit. And in the end, the goal is peace among allies.

An enemy is opposed to your interests; he wants you weak. What is to your advantage is ultimately to his disadvantage. Your strength takes away from his power, making him feel either threatened or envious. If these feelings are intense enough, there will be an assault. Attacking enemies are determined to repossess your resources for their own use. There is no respect of your boundaries or perspective, but only a determination to dominate and control. There may be careful attention paid to you, but it is only to study your weaknesses and exploit them. He invites your confidence. The more you reveal about your thoughts, emotions, dreams, and vulnerable points, the better he understands how to take advantage of them. Enemies do not have any genuine interest in you personally. The goal is only your complete annihilation or absorption into their purposes.

An enemy's idea of peace is peace for himself, which means the absence of your interference (i.e. voice) and resistance. In essence, he wants to be in control without it appearing so. The pressure is pushed along as peace, but the compromise is not toward equal consideration but toward your submission without objection. You are expected to trust without questioning. Whatever promises he gave you to get you invested will gradually be dropped until he is master: you are burdened with heavy obligations to him, while he has no genuine consideration for you. It is an emotional "taxation without representation." In the end, he only wants to be in charge.

If an enemy can obtain his objective without a fight, this is clearly to his advantage. The less fuss, the better. Breaking down walls is tedious work; better to find an easier way in without so much trouble. If he looks innocent, maybe he can avoid detection. It is the Trojan Horse war strategy, and if done with cleverness, it will be very successful. But the tell-tale sign is that friends respect your boundaries, where enemies are determined to penetrate them. In this way, manipulation is like a spy. He sneaks in under the pretense of being an ally with the intention to help you, when actually his help does far more harm. Your judgment of his loyalties should not be based on personal magnetism, rhetoric, or ease of nature, but on the solid effects of his actions. If they are not at all for the greater good of your cause, then look deeper. It is an enemy, not an ally, who entirely squeezes out your interests and oversteps your boundaries. Do not neglect these or it may lead to the complete defeat of your purposes and ideals.

In this hostile environment, you have a fight. If you do not recognize this, you are already losing it. Regardless of what you contributed to the problem, there is aggression, and it cannot be lightly disregarded without serious consequences. Though you may be forced to engage the battle, your purpose in the war should still be peace. Peace cannot always be achieved peacefully, though. There are some weeds too deeply rooted to be simply pulled up; they must be dug up—which inevitably disturbs all the soil and vegetation nearby. Unfortunate but unavoidable. Superficial solutions will only leave the problem to grow deeper and stronger. War, in this case a mental one, may be the only course.

As personal as it may seem, the battle is really more against lies and the temptation to believe them than against your oppressor. The source of the lies, of course, is a huge factor, and all efforts should be directed at studying his technique and devising strategies against it. However, the end goal is to destroy the true enemy: the lies. Hopefully in the process, the truth will be made clear, and your oppressor can be rescued from himself. Of course, this is pure optimism, but not completely impossible. Keeping this goal in mind, however, will help to keep you from attacking the person (though you will freely be attacked personally) and concentrate on taking down the deceptions themselves.

Dangers of Not Engaging the Fight

Manipulation is determined to use you. And if you cannot leave, the only way to stop it is to fight back. The shift in thinking from fixing a problem to fighting against it is no easy task. But by failing to fight, or at least not offering any resistance, you allow manipulation to grow worse. Giving him the benefit of the doubt rather than trying to clear your doubt leaves him at liberty to become even more skilled at creating illusions. It gives him more time to draw others into the tricks, more techniques for keeping you silent and burdened, more confidence that his methods are perfectly fine and normal. As necessary as it might seem to keep the peace as long as possible, it is more necessary to fight. As hopeful as you might be that someone from the outside will notice and step in, you cannot afford to wait. Begin to dress for battle.

It's a Game

Manipulation is a game. The pawns are people's hearts, and his goal is absolute victory. On his part, rules are free to change without consequence. On your part, you must play fair. It is not a pleasant scenario, but it is even worse if you do not realize what is happening. Even if you do come to suspect that things are not quite right, it is still difficult to know what to do about it, especially if you cannot just walk away. Games are not so fun when the stakes are this high.

There are three obvious reactions to these unfair standards: 1) refuse to play, 2) complain, or 3) try to compromise. Instinctively, you know any battle with a manipulator will be nasty, so it is reasonable to try other approaches first. But if the manipulation is at all skilled or established, these are obstacles he can adroitly skirt around. Refusal is countered with accusations and burdens of guilt, complaints are met with confusing counterarguments, and compromise might begin well but will end badly. You end up just wearing yourself out running around in circles. Trying to play fair when the rules are rigged against you is exhausting.

If you remain unaware of the driving manipulation, trying to figure out the dynamics and the rules of this strange game is baffling. No amount of effort on your part seems to make things better. So you may find yourself reluctantly playing it and continually losing. It could be tolerable if it were only a game, but the cost of losing is pieces of your identity: first just your comfort; then your priorities, your confidence, your strength; then your peace, your joy, your purpose, and even your sanity. Whatever you might have done wrong in your life, it certainly does not deserve the silent and steady usurping of your dignity. This game is serious and needs to be taken so. All that is most sacred is under fire, and that is exactly why you must engage this. Once you have become convinced of that, you will have to set aside your repulsion of it, roll up your sleeves, and learn to play the game well enough to change the rules.

The hard truth is that anyone manipulating you hates you. But it is not often with hot, flaring anger; it is more with a cold, calculating contempt. He believes that you are beneath dignity and fair consideration and that you are worthless enough to be used. He demonstrates this with his scorn for your opinions, thoughts, emotions, and requests. His easy assumptions and unreasonable expectations show that you are not at all important as an individual. It is a cruel hatred that is far more intellectual and willful than emotional. Love might be freely expressed, but without respect, it is a lie. The relationship is not building you up but destroying you. It is not life-giving but blood-sucking. Enough is enough.

If something is clearly not right, it is time to start asking questions. It is time to study the problem as scientifically and objectively as possible. Collect evidence and draw logical conclusions from it. This is your safeguard. Manipulators toy with emotions, so how you feel is not such a reliable gauge just now. Lean on reason, objective standards, just consequences, and proven reality instead. Truth is your friend, and you must do everything in your power to uncover it. Firstly, for yourself.

2
RECONNAISSANCE

BEFORE ENTERING INTO A BATTLE, you need to be certain that you are fighting for a worthwhile cause. You must be fully convinced in your own mind that the enemy is real and dangerous. You must have exhausted all the other possibilities for achieving peace. You must believe that what you have to gain is more valuable than what you might lose. Before you invest anything else, your will must be set. It is a significant commitment, and you must be sure. With mind games, alas, this often takes years. Meanwhile, the root of power grows broader and deeper. So the sooner you can muster the courage to think boldly, the greater the hope.

Motivation to Unmask

Unmasking manipulation is a process, largely done in your own mind first. It is an unraveling of a thought process that is partially dominated by a subjectivity that is not your own. The goal is to bring you back to certain absolutes, where you have a greater chance of having clear judgment. This in turn gives you a confidence and boldness, which will frankly terrify the manipulator. Once this objectivity is well-mastered, then you are free to relax into a healthier form of subjectivity that is self-designed and self-expressive. Your opinions and experiences are beautiful. They are wonderful. They matter. It is just that, if you are being manipulated, they are a bit tangled with someone else's agenda right now. Completely separate first, then express.

Manipulation needs to be shown for the sham that it is. Not that you should go looking for flaws, but if they keep arising with no satisfactory explanation and addressing the issue has failed, it is time to unmask. Unveiling manipulation is a bit like pulling away the layers of an onion. Once you begin, you might be surprised by how complicated it is and how much cover-up may actually be happening. You will find that the role of others around you is significant and that normal niceties do not stand up to the strain of these dynamics. What seems to be often is not. By honorably serving the appearances, you are unknowingly feeding secret agendas—agendas that often entrap and enslave you even more. No matter how attractive the presentation, the end results can be devastating. And if it is done with any skill, any onlookers will be completely unaware.

It's About Control

Manipulation is psychological tyranny. Tyranny gives its selfish interest a higher value than it actually has and then forces others to uphold this false value. The motivation to support these topsy-turvy priorities often lies in threats. The underlying control is obvious in physical tyranny, where the body takes the beatings and the signs of suffering themselves are visible. You conform to another's will despite your own, and it is repulsive. When the game is isolated to the mental level, however, the threats are subtle, the heart is what is ill-used, and the suffering can easily go undetected for decades. The cooperation is still unwilling, just not noticeably so. His will looks like your choice. His control looks like your cooperation. This is the manipulation game.

With a manipulator, there is a distinct lack of character and empathy. A particular agenda is glorified in his own mind as being above respecting others. Though there may be words to make it appear he is thoughtful, when it comes to choosing between what is considerate of you and what is to his advantage, he will choose to his advantage—regardless of how much trouble it causes those who have already made great sacrifices for him. There may be gifts to justify his sincerity, but they will invariably be on his terms. If you press hard enough, you will find that they are really exaggerated, ostentatious, have strings attached, or offer him some self-benefit. They are not meant to bless you at all. There may be a great deal of style, but it is completely void of substance; the words are impressive, yet there is no real demonstration of the strong character that they suggest.

While most of us suffer with moments of anxiety, frustration, or doubt, which drive us to violate others' boundaries at times, in retrospect, there is generally some remorse for failing to show respect. Manipulation has no such remorse. People, as resources, are viewed more as a means to an end. They are useful tools for achieving his own ambitions. Resources may require some investment to keep them in working order, but they most certainly do not have any voice or influence themselves. Treating people this way is universally repugnant, though, if it is detected. In order to evade detection, there must be distractions from his true motivation. So it is a game of illusions.

If there are illusions, there is already a good understanding of what is ideal. If he knows enough of what good character looks like to feign it, he knows what is right. If he knows human nature enough to subtly twist the situations to get an advantage over others, he is aware of how dignity works. Regardless of whether he believes in mutual respect, he knows what it looks like. He must give enough to feed the illusion, but not enough that it will cost him anything valuable. It is crucial that he appears normal, respectable, and believable. Manipulation knows what right looks like but chooses not to rise up to do it in any genuine way. There is no ignorance about it. It is a choice. And it opts for the shortcut of control.

Control is an attack on respect. You, rather than being left to discover or express yourself, are driven down a path of someone else's choosing. The obvious forms of control illustrate this clearly. A gun pointed in your back will compel you to do any number of things you might not otherwise do. It is when the control is happening in the mind more than in the body, that it is far more difficult to identify. But the effects are very much the same. Because the causes are more difficult to recognize, they often go unaddressed for years—even worsening with time. This, in fact, can do far more damage than isolated physical intimidation. The obvious control is obviously wrong. The subtle control is not so obviously wrong, so it may be continually overlooked by all parties. This is precisely what manipulation wants to happen. The less you see, the more you can be mastered.

After being repeatedly manipulated, there develops an unspoken understanding. You may be superficially free to make your own decisions, but if they are not the ones that he wants you to make, there will be consequences. This threat is generally covert, though, because the consequences are attacks against inner immeasurable qualities: dignity, peace, self-respect, self-confidence, hope. These are the unnoticeable pieces of your person. But the attacks are real nevertheless, however subconscious. And they are significant factors to weigh in making decisions. With the safety of your core being at stake, you may begin to automatically choose based not on what is best but on what will avoid his attacks. So intense pressure drives the victimized, and there is no evidence to prove it. Elegant to the core.

What is behind these dynamics is an underlying fear of offending the manipulator. While most of his associates may not realize it is a fear, they will hesitate to offend him. Though they may not fully know why and their reasoning may be dressed up with other justifications, ultimately they are afraid of him. He knows how to press their wills, how to compel them to choose to do something that is not quite right, how to play the situation to his own advantage and to their shame. Understandably, people do not like to be caught in this sort of discomfort. They will likely take extreme measures to avoid a confrontation with him, because instinctively they know that the easier route is to endure some uneasiness of mind rather than to try to change his. Treat him gingerly and you will not get burned… And this fear is exactly what is fueling manipulation's tremendous power.

Weighing the Evidence

Weighing motivations is a precarious business. But when you are dealing with hidden agendas and artificial fronts, it is your best safeguard to test the waters before jumping in. The subtle little things, which are often casually dismissed, do speak truth. Listen to them carefully, and you will have a far better understanding of how you stand. The less integrity, the more deceit. As far as you are able, dig up the truth. Motivation means everything. Good intentions honestly look for the most universal good first and eventually find it. Bad intentions look for short-sighted, self-benefit first and find it at the expense of others. If the only thing that answers the evidence is a selfish motivation, then the motivation is likely selfish.

Manipulation's goal is to get you to move. If you can look beyond the tricks and see the situation from his perspective ("How can I play this to my advantage?"), it really is not so hard to debunk. A complete lack of integrity may be hard to believe, but once you come to accept that his conscience is corrupted, it really is not so difficult to unmask. You know that the thought process is all about gaining an upper hand. Whatever it takes to get that advantage is fair game; what is not to his advantage is dropped. Your weaknesses are exploited while his are disguised. Regardless of how the actions are presented, what is actually happening is selfish to the core.

But of course, first you must be convinced that the tricks are actually deceptive ploys. Depending on the skill of the deceiver, this may come only after being repeatedly stung by them. Trying to persuade even intelligent people of an illusion is tedious, and unless it is done with prolonged, calm insistence, it may do more harm than good. It is far more important to convince yourself than to convince anyone else, however. In the end, character will show itself to be what it is. It really does not need much help from you, but you must step out of the way to give it that opportunity. Covering up his shame, scrambling to prevent disasters, and looking for reasonable explanations for unreasonable behavior all block truth. Leave the evidence alone to be discovered, and the right conclusion will naturally follow—eventually.

A few basic questions might help to clarify a situation:

- Does he demand respect without offering it?
- Is there a continual shifting of standards or lines of argument when circumstances change?
- Is there a strong insistence on an ideal that is never realized?
- Is he adept at erecting his own boundaries while refusing to recognize those of others?
- Are there other unspoken double standards?
- Is he more interested in proving himself right or in making things right?
- Are his arguments more for his rights or for universal good?
- Is mercy expected without any being offered?
- Beyond the presentation, where do the shame, blame, and fame actually fall?
- If you confront him with a wrong he has done, are you offered an apology or a dismissal?
- If you pull away from him, does he let you go out of respect or apply more pressure to keep you obligated?
- Do his closest associates know a "dark side" of him that he does not reveal to the general public?
- At his funeral, would you be more grieved or relieved?

It is vital that you make these judgment calls. What he claims must be consistently confirmed by his behavior. You must play the judge. You must know where you stand, not only for the sake of self-preservation but also for the greater good. Support your allies; defend against your enemies. In the end, the suppression of human freedom and dignity does no one any favors. Unearth the evidence, make fair judgments from it, and choose wisely your course of action. And through it all, you need to concentrate on keeping yourself strong and grounded in reality.

The Transformation

Manipulation draws people in with visions of grandeur. But you will find that the longer you are under the spell, the less the bright promises satisfy. It *was* too good to be true, no matter how true it did seem. Unfortunately, this is nearly impossible to judge from the start. Talented illusionists make their tales believable. But with time, their victims slowly come to suspect the truth. They find themselves progressing through a transformation of policy. From enthusiastic support to bold resistance, most of the people under the influence are at various points along the spectrum:

Eager cooperation: This is a whole-hearted belief in the vision as it was eloquently presented, with an eagerness to support it in self-sacrifice. There is an absolute confidence in the goodness of the portrayed cause.

Willing cooperation: This comes from people who are willing to help support the vision, though they still want to hold to their personal interests as far as possible.

Reluctant cooperation: This is a form of indulgence from those who feel obligated to cooperate but would rather not. They are generally looking for a strong enough excuse to get out of it.

Cooperation out of fear: This cooperation is driven strictly by fear of what will happen if they do not cooperate. Their personal beliefs are not worth the trouble their resistance would cause.

Tolerance: This is only an option to those who are not entangled in the manipulation. It is a reluctance to take a stand of any kind.

Passive resistance: Initially, this may be attempted by respectfully voicing your concerns. Ultimately, it is demonstrated by simply declining to cooperate. There remains a degree of lingering doubt, respect, or fear in this, however.

Active resistance: This is a determination to undermine manipulation's purposes, which have proven to be definitively bad.

Violent resistance: This engaging of the battle is a full commitment to fight an evil with all the resources available. There is an absolute confidence in the ill of the true cause.

Learning is a part of life. Changing and refining are signs of growth. Unhappily, when things are not as they seem to be, the journey can be unpleasantly rocky. Unfortunate as it may be, some fights must be engaged. So if you are at the final breaking point, prepare to fight! The cause is worthwhile. But know that you will likely not be heartily supported. If the deceit is at all pervasive, others on the journey of enlightenment are not as far along as you are. They might not understand the extreme measure you will have to take. Rise up in resistance anyway.

War Strategy

Battling with innocence involves far less finesse but far greater strength of character than manipulation does. But it will require clear sight and a clear head. If you are trapped in manipulation, however, getting to that point is in itself a battle. You must come out from under the influence as much as possible so that your judgments can be clearer, your actions can have more purpose, and you can get your footing. You need to be prepared to fight well if you must fight such a seasoned warrior. You must have strategy and resources, as well as a strong conviction of the justice of your cause. But also you must fight nobly. The ultimate intent of all just war must be to establish peace.

The goal is mutual dignity and respect, not domination. Regardless of the mean tricks the opposition is playing, you fight the good fight.

There is a progression to this. Steps need to be carefully taken in their proper order. It is important to do each well, without rush. Rush is a type of pressure that will only increase the difficulty of the later steps. Manipulation is enough pressure without adding your own. Yet there must be steady progress—maybe not day by day, but certainly month by month.

1. **Identify the problem.** Learn from your pain and shame. Be specific. Begin to observe the dynamics, cause and effect, behavioral patterns, and ultimate outcomes. The more precisely you can identify what is happening, the more effectively you can counteract it. Know what you are up against.

2. **Know yourself.** This includes identifying what you might be contributing to the problem. (Passivity is not a neutral stance but a significant contribution to manipulation.) Know what your weaknesses are and how you are vulnerable. But also know your worth. You must believe that you have legitimacy as a human being, with valid dignity, perceptions, and emotions that should not be continually disregarded. Sort through the hurt and any coping mechanisms that you have been using. Discard what has proven to be unbeneficial.

3. **Embrace reality.** Accept that things are not going to get better on their own. Let go of the ideal he feeds to keep you giving. Know what is right and stand up for it.

4. **Establish a better strategy.** Get prepared to fight. Get strong. Create space. Get support. This may include improving your resources or opportunities. It always requires coming out from what is familiar. And it most certainly means changing your mindset.

5. **Engage the battle.** Use what you have come to understand to fight for what you see as right and good.

6. **Let go.** Leave behind what is no longer necessary. Your old purpose, coping methods, pain, identity, and mentality, all must be left behind to make room for the new. Even the anger over the injustice must eventually be left behind. Shed all the lingering mentalities and baggage of the past.

7. **Move on.** Embrace your new freedoms and develop the new strengths that you need to keep moving forward into a bright future.

Revisiting steps is necessary and important. This journey is a continual one, though it will get easier with practice. Manipulation is a mighty difficult beast to conquer, so coming back to refocus on your purpose or identity, to refuel your strength, or to adjust your strategy are all necessary at times. And let go and move on as much as you can, as far as you can, as soon as you can. As paradoxical as it may seem, rising opposition is a good sign of progress. Keep pressing for what is good. Begin with understanding.

3
THE TRICKS: COERCION

MANIPULATION IS BASED ON LIES, albeit subtle ones, but lies nonetheless. Therefore, there is no full disclosure or frank authenticity that might reveal truth, but only a bag of tricks. You might have an inkling that something low is going on, but until you can actually prove it, he will still have the upper hand in the relational dynamics. So what you need is more than suspicion; it is objective evidence. The important thing, though, is to convince yourself. For now, outsiders are a distraction and a hindrance to your investigation. Seek clarity for yourself, enough clarity to give you a firm conviction that something unfair is indeed happening. Collect enough evidence to convince yourself, not necessarily to win a case. Because once you know, you are the one who will need that confidence to boldly confront the tricks.

This is no easy task. Manipulation plays off of subtleties. It plays its tricks on a deep level while ensuring that the superficial appearances and arguments are good. That means you are going to have to dig a little deeper, too. If you are not in a position to just walk away from the game, then you will have to learn to play it shrewdly.

If he knows it well enough to regularly dupe you, then you need to know it well enough to spot it quickly, call him out on it, and demand a higher standard. This can be a daunting task, especially when your confidence, support, and strength may already be weak. But it can be done, and the first step is just to watch and think—no definite action required.

Manipulation plays its games on two fronts: coercion and confusion. Coercion is what he uses to get you to move. Though it may be contrary to your own best interest and judgment, somehow he convinces you to give. It may be a gift of resources, time, attention, support, or strength—some sort of investment of yourself. But with coercion, it ends up that the gift only benefits him. Confusion muddies the waters so you cannot see clearly enough to battle the coercion effectively. Skilled manipulators use them both boldly and effortlessly, so it can feel natural or seem reasonable. But it is not. Step back and analyze how he is getting what he wants from you.

Manipulators have a whole bag of tricks, sly and subtle. Before you can fight them effectively, you will need to know them as well as they do. So you need to pay careful attention, picking apart the nuances, to discover what is really happening. Knowing what you need to look for gives you an important advantage. The following are twenty-three common tactics of coercion. Undoubtedly, there are hundreds of variations, but these are a good overview of the tricks, why they work, and what can be done to counteract their effects. Come to know them well, because if you are encountering them in daily life, they will pounce on you artfully and unexpectedly. You must be ready to recognize and meet them head-on.

Methods of Coercion

1. Guilt Play (Moral Blackmail)

"Give or you will be acting against a good thing (love, gratitude, loyalty, justice, your duty, God's will, my rights, etc.)"

Most of us have some moral standard that we are willing to uphold despite a little discomfort to ourselves. That is indeed what good people do: sacrifice a little of themselves for a greater good. A manipulator keys into that in you. He will notice what you are passionate about, enough to sacrifice for. Then it is just a matter of dressing up his agenda in your passion. Voila! You give selflessly, and he reaps the rewards. Maybe the ideal was upheld by your sacrifice and maybe it wasn't; usually there is no way of verifying it either way. But he is satisfied, and you are left with an indistinct pang.

> *Mr. and Mrs. Anderson had an argument that ended in Mrs. Anderson moving back in with her parents. Mr. Anderson talks her brother into going over to reason with her. He argues, "A family needs to be together to work things out. By supporting her, you would be acting against the institution of marriage, you would not be promoting peace, and you would be failing to show me any mercy. You need to do something to help bring her back home where she belongs." The brother believes in marriage and family, peace and mercy, so resignedly, he goes to take up his brother-in-law's cause.*

Moral blackmail uses our sense of obligation to an ideal to get us to give. The key to coming out from under this is to see the bigger picture. Goodness is not an isolated set of ideals, some of which you choose to uphold. Rather it is an integrated web of principles that are woven together to create goodness. Goodness needs mercy *and* justice, faith *and* wisdom, compassion *and* boundaries. Step back and judge for yourself what is more necessary to achieve the greatest good, then act accordingly. And know, you have absolutely **no** obligation to justify yourself for refusing to give.

2. Pity Play

"Give or you will cause me great suffering or needless temptation."

Pity play is designed to trigger your sympathy. Individuals aren't perfect, and they do need some leeway and understanding. People of goodwill believe this and want to relieve suffering, give strength, and ease hardships in life. They want to help. So by the manipulator appearing needy, you are more inclined to give generously. Presented with drama and some mixed truth, the plea can be *very* convincing. Only the need is greatly exaggerated and feeding it only ends in things getting worse.

Rob has been assigned Kyle as a lab partner ever since school started, even though all the other students have switched three times already. Kyle is very difficult to work with and sometimes unsafe. Rob is tired of cleaning up his messes and doing all of the work, so he mentions this to his science teacher. The answer he gets is, "I know he's not easy to work with, but you know if I assign him as a partner to anyone else, there's going to be endless complaining. Just make the best of it, kid." Rob doesn't want to make things hard on his teacher, so he keeps at it.

The benefit to pity is that it naturally wears thin. You may be drawn in the first time or two, but eventually if nothing changes for the better, it is spent. Let it be. He has lost your trust. If he were really concerned about the suffering to begin with, he would have tried other solutions before burdening you. Abandon the pity. A manipulator will then move onto different ploys or different players, but allow your immunity to this one sink in, without any guilt.

3. Shame Game

"Give or I will expose your shame, stripping you of respect and dignity."

The shame game is just blackmail. It threatens to expose your shame unless certain conditions are met. Pure blackmail states the threat outright—you know what will happen if you do not comply. Playing off of people's shame is the same except the threat is only implied. Often situations are cleverly devised so that you are placed in an awkward or embarrassing situation—one that is too personal or tedious to explain. The only ready option for covering the embarrassment is sacrificing something else.

Molly is in the middle of spring cleaning and handwashing. The apartment she shares with her brother is in an upheaval, with personal items all over. Then her brother, Marcus, shows up with a carload of friends, knowing she is in the middle of a mess. He insists they are coming in to hang out. Molly is appalled, but Marcus will not leave. She suggests they go bowling or something. Marcus insists they have no money. If she wants them to leave, she will have to spot them. Molly reluctantly pays out.

Often in the midst of this, there is a sense of its injustice, but the only options for handling it are to create a scene, argue, or walk away in silent protest—all of them shaming to some extent. To give or not to give, that must be your snap decision. Is the gift or the shame more costly?

Unfortunately, prevention is your best defense. Avoid vulnerability with this individual. Guard your weaknesses. Get strong enough so the shame he dumps onto you will not crush you.

4. Appeal to Pride

"Give, unless you are mastered by some inferior emotion [e.g. fear, anger, greed, jealousy]."

This tactic is a sophisticated version of the childhood dare. His accusations are offensive, and you must do what he suggests in order to disprove them. When our pride is bristled, we tend to act more impulsively to protect our dignity and can be too distracted to notice that we are being set-up. So we readily give without thinking it through and find that was really his objective all along. And so we pay the bitter price of being the fool rather than looking like one.

Sandra and Hugh were assigned to work together on a corporate project. Sandra took the lead and left all the tedious labor to Hugh, who did his best. In presenting it, Sandra then took all the credit. Hugh pulled her aside afterward and objected, but she laughed him off. "You aren't so petty, are you? It's not like you got paid any less for doing the easy parts, so what's your beef?" So Hugh bit his tongue.

Subtly, he has reduced the situation to two options: you must give or be considered as weak. Ideally, you would recognize this and walk away. Reject the sense of inferiority he has created. Do not give a reason why you are choosing otherwise, though you might suggest it is far more than his simplistic one. Stall if necessary. Buy some time to think it through thoroughly. The more you can step back from what a manipulator is saying, the safer you will be.

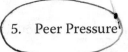

5.   Peer Pressure

"Give or I will ensure that popular opinion is solidly against you."
"Give or you will completely disappoint all these people who are depending on you."
"Give. People you respect say you should."

Peer pressure comes from our desire to belong and be accepted and often influences our decisions more than we realize. Reputation is a powerful force; how we are viewed by others does matter and should be valued. What other people think, especially those whom we respect, does carry weight. If you are isolated or regularly manipulated, this desire for acceptance and normalcy is even stronger. You may value them as your anchor just to keep you sane, so the threat of losing that connection to dignity is even more potent.

> *Abby has been struggling in her marriage to Drake and suggests they go see a marriage counselor. Drake resists. Among other arguments, he says, "You're going to go talk about this with our friends, I'm sure, and what are they going to think? That we can't handle our own problems, that's what. Well, I can, and I'll make sure everyone knows that you are the problem here." Abby knows Drake's charming and persuasive nature would be sure to sway their friends' opinions. So she drops it and now doesn't dare to see a counselor for herself, either.*

Though the temporary loss of respect may seem overwhelming at the time, ultimately choosing what you believe is right will win far deeper respect. Firstly, work for a self-respect and then from others who come to see what is really happening. It takes boldness and courage to step out, believing that truth will eventually be made known and good people will arise to help. The threat might seem real, but it is only a bluff. Most people are more reasonable than you might suppose and will look deeper if you have given them a reason to...defy their supposed conclusions and give them reason to.

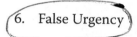

6. False Urgency

"Give or there will be a terrible disaster! Hurry! There isn't much time!"

Urgency requires rapid reaction rather than careful thought. When there is a crisis, you are more likely to spontaneously give to avoid a mess rather than step back and analyze the situation. This is exactly the conditions that manipulators want, making it easy to lead you down a road of their own choosing. In order to make it believable, though, you must be drawn into the anxious atmosphere. Especially if there is no true urgency, the manipulator must create frenzy by their own behavior. After all, panic is contagious.

Mr. Hardin rushed into Jane's office in a hysteria. "I just found out the auditor is coming tomorrow. With Lynnette out of the office, the books aren't up to date and the office is still a mess from remodeling. I need you to stay tonight to get this done." Jane is willing to help out and agrees. But when five o'clock comes around, she sees Mr. Hardin happily going home for the night, and her with four more hours of work to do.

Your best defense is to be vigilant, to think, and to continually question. Real crises absolutely do need your help, but artificial ones absolutely should not have it. Take a step back to assess the real need before investing into a sacrificial rescue. Find out what is driving the crisis and why it is so urgent. Change the tone of the hype by remaining calm and collected. And then offer alternative solutions, preferably ones that will remove you from the equation. The urgency generally dissolves when you focus more on finding a good solution rather than rushing to the relieve the problem on his terms.

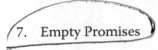

7. Empty Promises

"Give and I will give in return."
"Give just this time and things will be so much better."
"Give and God will reward you for it because you are doing the right thing."

Empty promises are just lies. Though they might sound sincere at the time, the end result proves there was no intention to uphold the promise from the beginning. A manipulator gives the appearance of a fair trade and then makes no effort to uphold his end of the bargain. The lie raises your hopes, energizing your giving, and then ends abruptly. If there is any recompense for your sacrifice, it is only minimal. The hopes are never realized and the expectations that were raised are lightly dismissed. Again, it was just about getting you to move.

Connie, the teacher in charge of prom, stopped into Chloe's art room and said, "I really need you to help out with the decorations this year. You have the artistic eye and always do such a nice job." Chloe hesitated, so Connie added, "The students will so appreciate it. I'll own you one." That was five years ago. Chloe still puts her all into putting up and taking down the decorations as Connie directs, but she has yet to have any favor returned. But Connie keeps insisting (though Chloe has never heard herself) that the students appreciate her work so much.

This type of coercion is best prevented. Trying to extract his part of the bargain from him after the fact just leads to a tangle of other manipulative tactics and rarely gains you anything. Accept the loss and learn to clearly establish any agreement ahead of time—with specific details, limits, and timelines. This might feel a little legalistic, but there is no shame in protecting your investments. Better still is to avoid all agreements. Those who have no shame in making empty promises have no shame in applying other forms of deceit. They are not worth your energy.

8. Extreme Projections

"Give, because if you don't, this will happen, and then this, and then this...
It will be a disaster! You will be sorry."

Similar to false urgency, extreme projections play off of your fears. It generates a picture of tragedy as a result of a chain reaction, starting with your refusal to give. Though no immediate negative result can be foreseen, there is some grave potential that he highlights more than any other. Certainly, legitimate problems are best avoided at the start, but extreme projections are often far-fetched, relying more on drama than reality.

Cole and Katie are dating, and they have spent the last three evenings together. Cole has a big project at work that needs him to put in extra time, so he was planning on staying at the office tonight. Then Katie calls and asks what they are doing this evening. Cole explains that he'll be working late. "You can't!" says Katie. "The girls will find out and drag me out with them. You know they'll get me to drink too much, and I'll probably end up flirting with strangers—or worse. Please go out with me instead."

Leave the panic alone. Do not touch it. See enough that there are illegitimate fears at play that should not be entertained. Trying to settle imaginary worries is futile. Remote possibilities are hardly probabilities and should not be addressed until they become so. Deal with the issue if it becomes a legitimate problem. Until then, do not be lured into the frenzy.

9.   Devouring Expectations

"Give just a little and a little more and a little more and a little more..."

Devouring expectations draw you in by your desire to please. At first, it is just a little, so little that you hardly feel it. But then, what you gave was not enough—it will take just a little more. But then that isn't enough, either, until you find that the sum total of what you give ends up being far beyond what you initially planned and certainly far more costly. Somehow your initial generosity has raised the expectations far beyond what you meant. Bit by bit, your resources were stolen.

Quentin enjoys working on cars and agrees to take a look at his neighbor, Charlie's, vehicle, which has been leaking oil lately. Charlie stops by to watch. Quentin finds that there is a simple fix, if he just puts it on his lift and invests twenty minutes into it. He thinks it is the neighborly thing to do, so he is glad to help. But then Charlie begins to hint at other problems (along with his money troubles): first the belt is squeaking, and then he remembers the radiator should be flushed, and then the tires should be rotated. Quentin finds his entire day devoured because he offered to help out a little.

The solution to devouring expectations is expressing a firm "no" and dropping them. If what you have already given does not satisfy him, he is not worth satisfying. You are not obligated to give beyond what you already have chosen to give. Draw the boundary when the gift begins to become uncomfortable. However rude it may feel, you must either ignore the plea or bring it out into the open. Getting them to express their expectations of you will generally reveal them to be unreasonable. Clarification will often reveal the unfairness.

10. False Extensions

"Give. You promised me this, and that implies this and this and this and this, too."

Similar to devouring expectations, false extensions exploit your vague commitments. Rather than asking, it presumes that your offer encompasses far more than you intended. If there was some room for misunderstanding, it is reasonable to give a little extra rather than create tension. But that isn't what is happening at all. By breaking what he really wants you to give into bite-sized pieces, you are not as likely to notice how much you end up giving until it is too late.

Dion offered to help his father with the yard this summer. Eagerly, his father accepted. But what started out as mowing once a week has turned into cleaning out gutters, repainting the shed, reseeding the lawn, trimming the shrubs, and helping to redo the landscaping. Dion reasons that these do qualify as yard work, but it turned into much more than he was prepared to do.

Awareness is your greatest asset. Once you notice that you are giving beyond your willingness, establish a boundary. Even if it is late in coming, put it in place anyway. It might feel unfriendly or uncompromising, but it is necessary. Anyone who will disregard common respect needs something firmer to guard against their appetites. And next time, make your commitments extremely clear.

11. Appeal to a Precedent

"Give, you did before."

This tactic relies on our desire to be consistent. Reliable and trustworthy people are stable and follow certain codes of conduct. By changing your course, the manipulator suggests that you would be admitting you were wrong before or that you are fickle and irresponsible. If you know that neither one of these cases is true, you may be tempted to give, just to prove that you are dependable.

> *Fran made the wedding cake for her niece's wedding several years earlier. Now her nephew is getting married. Fran is bogged down with work responsibilities, though, and was planning on getting something off of the registry. Her sister-in-law announces at the bridal shower, "Frannie's wedding gift is always the cake. You can count on her, dear. She does a phenomenal job." Showered with praise and gratitude, Fran resigns herself to making time somehow.*

A gift is a choice and ought to be understood as a one-time offer. It is your responsibility to yourself to weigh what you are able to give in any given situation. Circumstances change, and your choices must change with them at times. It is not your loyalties or priorities or character that is flawed, but the expectations others have placed on you. Drop the obligation as graciously as possible because it was never yours to begin with. Correct the presumption and move on.

12. Loaded Analogies

"Give. Look at it this way, if... then it would be obvious the right thing to do is to give."

Loaded analogies make a comparison between the current situation and another of the manipulator's choice. It is in his power which details are ignored and which are highlighted. Significant facts may be overlooked while other ones are exaggerated, so the situations end up looking astoundingly alike. Once he has you drawn in that they are essentially the same, he can easily lead you to conclude that the outcomes ought to be the same also: you should give.

> *There was a bear that had been terrorizing a neighborhood and badly mauled some backpackers. Some men from the town managed to corner it against a building and were about to destroy it when some women from the humane society came running. "Be merciful. Teddy Roosevelt had pity on a bear and became a great man because of it. Spare this one, too."*

Do not be drawn into the fantasy. Focus on the facts of the real situation and deal with them directly. Any sidetracking to different situations only clouds the current issue. Sort out what you have as it is, not as it is dressed up to be. If you are able, challenge the assumptions, and you may find the analogy is not so strong after all.

13. False Compromise

> *"What I want is this [dangerous, extreme, or irresponsible] thing. What you want is this [reasonable] thing. The compromise is therefore here [right where the most I could realistically get is anyway]."*

Compromise is about finding a middle ground where both parties must give a little so that both can end up with some of what they wanted. There is a sense of fairness and equity about it, and reasonable people are willing to concede a few points for the sake of mutual peace. But once a manipulator is involved, the compromise usually does not end up so equable. False compromise uses the haggling trick of asking for more than you really want so that the "compromise" ends up being more to your advantage. By boldly demanding an excessive amount (often with great detail and relentless insistence), it appears that he is giving up just as much as you are. In reality, however, he hasn't given up much of anything except a lot of empty demands, while you are left with nearly nothing.

> *Daniel and Marsha are married and discussing a budget. Marsha wants to take a cruise, remodel the kitchen, and upgrade the swimming pool. Daniel thinks that they should save up to replace the roof and the septic system. Marsha suddenly confides in Daniel all her secret hopes for adding on an extra bedroom, trips to Europe, and expensive jewelry. But all she is asking is for a few kitchen upgrades and a week vacation. Daniel prays that the septic system will hold out a little longer.*

False compromise preys on our sense of fairness. It exploits our sense of justice to its own advantage. If possible, walking away from the situation to regain your bearings is best. Make a chart. Clarify the difference between needs and wants. Prioritize. Try to reduce the argument to one of facts and figures rather than desires and emotions. Appeal to a third party. The extreme requests need to be shown to be completely unreasonable and therefore not worth consideration. This will require firm resolution and some tedious effort, but it is your only hope toward finding a genuine compromise.

14. False Options

> *"You can give me A, B, or C... Oh, wait, B and C won't work out. Oh well, give me A, then."*

This appears to be a gesture of respect, at first. Especially in the midst of manipulation, being offered a free choice is deliciously close to being offered freedom and dignity. It is much welcomed and often eagerly accepted; only things do not turn out exactly like you chose. Somehow your choices become too impossible, and you find that your option was no option at all. You do not really have a voice; it was only an illusion.

> *Daniel and Arnold are roommates. Daniel convinces Arnold to help host a party at their apartment by promising him that it will be quiet with just be a few people and that Arnold can invite his closest friends also. So Arnold dutifully attends to the bulk of the preparations. Then suddenly Daniel's friends invite more friends, and the party becomes quite an event. Daniel explains it wasn't his fault and that it all just happened. The party gets large and rowdy. Arnold finds not only are his friends not welcome, but neither is he.*

Even if it makes you feel suspicious, be wary. If you have lost your voice mysteriously when you thought you had one, it is time to start questioning the sincerity of the offer. You need to draw away from the prefabricated options set before you and create new ones, ones that include more to your benefit also. Stand your ground. If he is not willing to take your opinions seriously, then neither are you obligated to take his seriously. Draw a firm boundary and walk away.

15. Dropped Responsibilities

"I refuse [to rise up to my most basic responsibilities] unless you give."
"I'm going to do something very bad if you don't give enough to entice me to stop."

This tactic plays off of your sense of order and responsibility. It is likely the simplest of all manipulative tricks to perform because it simply requires the manipulator to refuse to do his most basic and understood duty. No amount of arguing or reasoning will help because it isn't about achieving the greatest good, but about him getting what he demands. Any sense of fairness, order, decency, safety, peace, or self-control may be suddenly disregarded, just to achieve his end. He will be a beast until you meet him on his terms.

Grandma is babysitting for the day and promised to take her three grandchildren to the movies. They are very excited until Gordon finds out Grandma is not going to buy them popcorn. It comes time to leave. At seventy pounds, Gordon refuses to get in the car and go to the movies. Grandma cannot lift Gordon, and his two sisters were so looking forward to the outing. Grandma wants to keep her word and reward the girls, but there seems no other way than by promising to buy them all popcorn. Suddenly, Gordon is agreeable to going.

Do not stoop to giving. Regardless of how much of a mess it might make, let it become a mess. Giving will only reinforce such behavior, adding to the chaos and irresponsibility. There are always more ways to become unpleasant, so there is no limit to how much he might come to demand. Though not always possible, leave him to suffer the consequences of his own irresponsibility. This might require shrewdness and boldness to isolate the consequences to the offender, but work toward that end. If others must suffer a bit by his irresponsibility, let it be. It is not your responsibility to order his chaos. Eventually he will be hated for it, as it should be.

16. False Generosity

*"Look! I am giving you this magnanimous [not] gift. So you must give
me this little [not] thing I want."*

False generosity can come in several forms. It may be an offer
to give you something that in reality is already yours: *"I will let you
take a nap tomorrow."* It may be something that is not really his to
give: *"My brother will set you up with a free meal at his restaurant."*
Or the value of what he is offering is just exaggerated: *"This faux
pearl bracelet was very special to my grandmother."* But whatever
the offer, it is built up to be a great gift for you, and expectations
are raised that you do something great in return. Generally, what is
expected, though, costs more than just your time or money; it often
costs a piece of your dignity. Because your gift is mostly intangible,
it is considered of little value. So in trading, you are made cheap.

*Sally's church was having a rummage sale, so she went to her
neighbors to ask for unwanted items they would be willing to
donate. They were very willing, and she was grateful. But now
she finds that anytime her neighbors clean out their attics or
garages, they leave their unwanted items on her porch. These
have become a burden for her to manage, and now the porch
looks trashy. Yet in return, they expect her to purchase a wide
assortment of overpriced items that their children regularly
sell door-to-door for fundraisers. Sally does not want to be
ungrateful, so she obliges despite her tight budget.*

False generosity plays off of your sense of reciprocity. Good
relationships require giving in both directions. But giving to get is
not really giving at all. You have no obligation to return a favor that
is not blessing you; rather return the gift. If there are going to be
unspecified strings attached to it, it is by far better to steer clear of

it entirely. Leave the accusations of being ungrateful or suspicious or unreasonable to fall to the side. If you have been treated unfairly before, there are no grounds for cooperation again. Walk away.

17. Bribery

"Give me this [significant] thing and I will give you this [cheap trinket]."

Similar to false generosity, bribery is an unequal trade. Rather than expecting to receive a return out of obligation, however, it is considered more as a business deal. It is stated up front that you are both giving and getting something. But bribery relies on the ignorance of one party; somebody is getting the short end of the deal without realizing it. It appeals to your desires, often deep ones that the manipulator suggests he can fulfill. But in the end, you are left empty.

Lionel works for an advertising firm. The president offers to create a new executive position for him. It comes with a big office, personal secretary, and a company car. He can choose the carpet and the car model. The salary is great, the view is fantastic, and there will even be a cappuccino maker. The hours he is expected to put in are not specified, however, and he cannot seem to get a straight answer.

Metaphorically, read the fine print. Whatever agreement you make that may be seriously binding needs to be thoroughly investigated. Rushing into an agreement in good faith may leave you trapped in a difficult position, possibly for years. While relational issues are generally not as binding, social forces can keep you bound, too. And with a manipulator, it is far easier to avoid his traps than to get out of them.

18. Withdrawal

"Give or I will cut off your communication/attention/affection with me."

This tactic appeals to our need for companionship but works only for close relationships. What the manipulator has to offer is seen as unique and vital. Whatever closeness that you might share with that person he is now threatening to withdraw from you. And so there arises a fear of loss or isolation, which might be unbearable.

Jen and Lise are sisters and dear friends who share a room. Lise wants to get a vanity, but it would take over part of her sister's space. Try as she might, Lise cannot convince Jen to give it up because she uses the extra floor space for reading. Lise concludes, "Forget it, you're not worth talking to," and gives her the silent treatment for a week. Jen decides she'd rather read on her bed and have her sister back than defend her floor space.

The withdrawal tactic proves to be ineffective if you are simply not bothered by it. The manipulator would really be doing you a favor by leaving you alone. But if the loss is felt keenly, then it is time to fill that void with people who are not going to treat you this way. Pouty fits do not deserve any attention and will eventually become too much of a strain to keep up. Indulging it, though, opens yourself up to repeat performances. Better to leave it untouched from the start.

19. Harassment

"Give [or I will see that you have no peace or rest]."

While the threat may not be stated, the actions themselves speak loudly enough. Nagging, pestering, whining, hounding, looming, lurking, stalking, lobbying. Harassment is designed to wear you away with its relentless insistence. Your peace is being attacked, and he has no shame in attacking it to get what he wants out of you. The deeper the individual can reach into your personal time or space, the more effective the method. He has every intention of driving you nuts. It is purposeful, and it is powerful!

Elaine's mother-in-law, Lois, has come to stay with them while she looks for a nearby house. Lois is critical of the way Elaine is raising their two children, though, and thinks they need more structure and social involvement. So Lois makes sure she is present whenever the children are interacting with Elaine, not-so-subtly commenting on her "errors." Then she starts leaving her articles on child-rearing and bringing the conversation around to it when visitors come. Elaine is nearly out of her mind and agrees to sign up the kids for karate and dance, just to silence Lois.

Ideally, you should shut them out—actually or metaphorically. Developing the tough skin it takes to ignore, blow off, or make a joke of these attacks takes a good reserve of confidence and some time to develop, though. If you are not there yet, then boundaries are your safeguard. Tell them to cut it out—frequently. Close a door or even lock it. Avoid contact. Hang up the phone, walk away. If it seems rude, it is only a response to a much ruder act. Ignore it. Erect whatever boundaries are necessary to protect your peace. They will be attacked; defend them staunchly anyway. Whatever it takes, put as much distance between you and him as possible.

20. Unjust Punishments and Disproportional Consequences

"Give or I will make certain that you are miserable and deny you resources."

This method is a threat to your sense of comfort and well-being. It is usually accompanied by angry outbursts, where the pretense of other coercion methods is too much bother. In his effort to regain control, he will spurn true justice to establish his own. The arbitrary or disproportional execution of punishment induces a terror that often leads people to "walk on eggshells" or hide at the first signs of the rising rage. It is nearly impossible to tell what the expectations are when consequences are harsh and the offense unclear.

Garrett comes home to his wife, young daughter, and toddler and notices a tiny button on the floor. He suddenly bursts into a rage, claiming that it is a choking hazard and why can't people take better care to keep the house clean. His wife and daughter quickly scramble to pick up the button and begin thoroughly sweeping the house to try to calm his anger, but then he threatens to throw away all the toys. The daughter is distraught, and his wife cannot reason with him. For the next several weeks, the wife and daughter are meticulous about trying to keep the house spotless, despite the odds with a toddler.

If you are faced with unjust punishments, the courageous thing to do is to bear them with dignity and fortitude. Know that they are unjust so that they do not weigh you down. There is likely something else going on that has nothing to do with you or your "offense." You still have to pay the price for it, though, but fighting back rarely accomplishes anything good. Persevering with calm and steady confidence is the strongest evidence of your innocence. Keep doing what is right despite the injustice. The contrast between your patient long-suffering and his malicious retaliation will make itself abundantly clear in time, without any help from you. Bear the heavy burdens but know *absolutely* that they are undeserved.

21. Intimidation

"Give or I will interfere with your freedom or physical safety."

Intimidation is founded on threats to physical freedom or safety, regardless of whether they are stated outright or not. These are likely the clearest violations of respect because there is a potential aggressive act. Somehow physical force or presence is being used to generate fear. Its purpose is to obtain something that otherwise would not be given. Intimidation has a large spectrum, however. It can be as obvious as severe physical attack with bruises and broken bones to as subtle as angry facial expressions. It may be in the form of threats, interrogation techniques, physical restraint, or psychological tormenting. Yet even for the more subtle forms, there is usually good reason to believe that a physical attack is likely; you are convinced that they would use the power they have over you if provoked. Intimidation only works if you believe there is a possibility of aggression. However subtle, the threat *is* real. There has been violence.

> *Andrew is a new driver, and his father is angry about a dent he found in the fender of the truck. Andrew knows his father put it there himself when he was backing their trailer the other day and considers mentioning this. But then he remembers, he has seen him kick their dog and pound on doors when he is angry. He has grabbed Andrew's shirt before and yelled in his face for far lesser things. If he thinks that Andrew put the dent in the truck, then he had better fix it without objection.*

Intimidation requires a firm and bold counteraction. The only useful means for dealing with it, as the prelude to violence, are fight or flight. Fear must be faced, either straight on or from a place of safety. Appeasement invariably fails. Patience only opens the opportunity for the situation to escalate. The sooner the problem is brought out into the open, the more hope there is for it to be properly handled. This usually involves risk, though. Plan carefully and act boldly. Reach out for help. Your freedom from fear is worth it. But please note: If there is violence involved, even in mild forms, it is no longer a matter of choosing not to be afraid but of getting to a place of safety.

22. Holding Others Hostage

"Give or I will ensure that [innocent] others suffer consequences."

The cruelest of all tactics, this exploits your love for others. Though often not stated, for then the evil nature of the threat would be abundantly clear, it is rather a pattern that is methodically established. If you do not give, you find that the wrath or manipulative tactics are spent on others nearby. They have to make up for the lack instead of you. And so it comes to be understood that others will suffer consequences if you do not comply. By doing nothing, you only watch the poison spread, knowing you had the power to stop it but you did not. This is unbearable, so the better option is to give.

Austin is in his early twenties and just moved out of the house to start his own roofing business. His two younger teenage brothers are still at home. His father calls Austin up to redo the roofs of the house and barns at their farm, at cost. Austin explains the business is new and he can't afford to do favors just now. His father is annoyed but then says, "Fine, fine. You don't want to help your family; I'll have your brothers do it." Austin objects, "They don't have any experience or the right equipment, Dad. It would be dangerous." His father answers,

"They'll learn. Everybody has got to start somewhere." So Austin scrambles to fit in his father's job.

Ideally, the key to protecting others is to keep them hidden. If you are aware of coercion occurring, it is best to create a haven. Withdraw into a safe place where you can develop meaningful relationships where the manipulator cannot reach. Keep your friends and confidences secret. They will become a vital source of strength if you need to take more drastic action later. Develop secret signals between coworkers. Hold secret conferences with your other family members. It may feel like a covert mission, but that is all right because you are under attack; this is war.

For dire situations, the answer might be for you to get out. Even if you have to leave those you love behind, strengthen them for the battle and withdraw. As long as there are no others to use as leverage, those left will be fighting for themselves. Without being hindered by the need to protect others, their fight can be more focused on abolishing the injustice.

23. By Momentum

"Give [or I will coerce you anyway]."

Disgust, fear, and exhaustion may lead to this final means of coercion. You know that he will get what he wants one way or another and going through the ordeal is just too much. Though the threats to being manipulated are not stated, you are keenly aware of their reality. It is far easier to just give him what he wants without all the games. It buys a temporary sense of peace and can avoid the feelings of confusion and shame that being tricked brings. The thing is, you are still giving what you would rather not.

Ruth is a new mom and is the only sibling living nearby her widowed mother. Her mother calls her up when the baby is three weeks old and says that since Ruth is on maternity leave, this is the perfect time for the three of them to take a road trip to visit her sister, fourteen hours away. Her mother has already made all the arrangements, and Ruth just needs to do most of the driving. The reasoning and excitement pours out before Ruth can say anything. By the time she could inject a response, she remembers that her mother invariably finds a way to get what she wants, and she doesn't feel like she could deal with all the pressure just now. She gives a non-committal, "Oh," which is taken as a "yes," and hopes that she can get some rest at her sister's house...

With coercion by momentum, the manipulation has reached its epitome with automatic compliance and effortless control. And you are utterly miserable. If you are aware enough to have gotten this far, then there is hope. You know there is a problem, and it is not still there because *you* haven't tried. It is time to use the strength you are saving in avoiding the coercion dance to begin to fight.

There are other tactics of a baser nature, including an appeal to jealousy, arrogance, vanity, greed, sensuality, or any number of other vices. Arguably, those who fall for these might deserve it. But the tactics are still present; there is still a subtle play on some deep desire or weakness that presses you toward a goal that is not of your own choosing. Of course, you may not be prone to all these tactics. Some may not bother you at all. But the nature of coercion dictates that the method is not important. It wants the effect—which is to press you into giving. A manipulator will apply many of these strategies. Those he finds most effective are well used. Those that do not work are discarded for better ones. And those individuals who do not fall into his traps are discounted as irrelevant or irreverent. The less you can be bothered, the less you can be coerced.

Giving is a vote of confidence; it is a way of showing that you believe in something. Coercion gets you to give for other reasons, taking with it a piece of your identity. Giving without believing is misleading, and in the end, he has gotten you to betray yourself. But manipulation is completely indifferent to this tremendous cost, and unless you learn to stop it, you may be paying it bit by bit until there is seemingly nothing left of yourself.

4
THE TRICKS: CONFUSION

COERCION WORKS BECAUSE it gets you to move, but coercion alone is not enough. If you are firmly grounded in reality and are reasoning, eventually you will catch onto the game. Even if you are not wise to all the particulars, you will figure out that something is not right and get fed up enough to walk away. So what the manipulator must do to keep you giving is to separate you from your grounding. Attention, clarity, good judgment, and reality must all be handicapped so that you cannot see what is actually happening. And so, he creates confusion.

Confusion introduces a strong uncertainty. And if there exists uncertainty, persuasion of any kind is much more effective. Manipulators thoroughly understand this and are willing to oblige by supplying any confusion necessary to stir up doubts. If we are no longer so confident in our abilities to judge rightly, even if just for an instant, this will have us second-guessing ourselves. This leaves us open to being led down a path of his choosing. Know what is happening so you are not drawn away.

The effectiveness of manipulation rests on how well he can

introduce chaos. This is a skill, but the best have mastered it so that it seems natural. Sometimes this will require careful conditioning of his victims over years, and sometimes it just needs a little charisma and finesse. But the common thread in the methods is boldness and confidence. The more confidently a manipulator introduces this chaos, the more likely people are to absorb it as normal. We must not see it as being awkward or unnatural, or we will not be taken in. Power plays are most effective when they go undetected.

Chaos is introduced along three main lines: diversion, distortion, and division. If attention is drawn to a problem, error, or weakness that threatens the manipulator's image or control, watch what he will do to avoid detection. Diversion draws attention away from the real problem to something else. Distortion changes the appearance of reality to something that is more helpful to the manipulator's purpose. Division simply separates you from your sources of strength and good judgment. All three attack truth.

Diversion

Diversion tactics create distractions. If the current topic is dangerously close to a truth that threatens his control, attention must be drawn away from it quickly. It is critical that the subject be dismissed, replacing it with another of more immediate interest. But he must do so without getting caught. Manipulation must not be discovered or its power will be shattered. Keeping people unaware is absolutely vital. And so skilled diversions will go completely unnoticed by the distracted parties. It seems the shift of attention was natural or at least unplanned.

Being aware of the tricks is the first step to overcoming them. You must be able to recognize what is happening before you can develop a strategy for counteracting them. You must see before you can be convinced, and you must be thoroughly convinced if you are going to be strong enough to battle them with all the agility they require.

Diversion Tactics

Changing the subject: A change of subject suggests a triviality about the original topic. If conversion is light, this is easy to do.

Creating a distraction: This can be applied with good results only by the most skilled. It creates some sudden, loud, and noticeable event to sidetrack attention. The idea is that the suddenness of the situation will break the flow of thought.

The fantastic offer: This is a distraction by grandeur. Something too good to be refused is offered to distract you from your original intent. It could be some amazing, tangible gift or even just a hot topic of conversation among those present. Whatever it is, the greatness of it overshadows further exploration of truth.

Initiating an aggressive offense: By the manipulator taking the initiative to make the first accusations, you are naturally left on the defensive. Regardless of how absurd the claims are, you are still left to scramble in defense—your attention is diverted from discovering truth. Even if you dare to offer a rebuttal, it will be weakened. The situation is then, at best, seen as a petty spat. Offering a counteraccusation means that you must fight a battle on two fronts: defending yourself *and* raising your complaint above his. Often people will decide that it is not worth the fight and let it go.

Driving a strong counterattack: If accused and caught off-guard, this is often the tactic manipulators use to create a distraction. By dramatically uncovering things (however ridiculous) that you might have to hide, attention is diverted from uncovering his guilty secrets. It offers an insistent and abundant flood of counteraccusations, certainly faster than you can disprove them. It is overwhelming. Quantity impresses, and it makes the process of disproving all the claims tedious or even impossible. Again, the issue is often dismissed as not worth the effort to untangle.

Undermining motivation or reasoning: This tactic challenges you to justify why you are even addressing the issue at all. You must thoroughly explain each step of your thought process, which, however strong, is not likely to be perfectly air-tight. And so, getting you to talk for long enough, you reveal a weak point that he can exploit. This attack implies that because your motivation or reasoning is not completely validated, your concern is irrelevant. Basically, he digs until he finds a way to make you seem foolish.

Emotional analysis: This tries to distract from the objective facts and justice of the situation to focus only on the emotional dimension. If the incident can be reduced to simply an emotional drama—how you are feeling about this—soothing talk is all that is needed to resolve the difficulty. The subtle implication being that there is not a real problem—you are just worked up about nothing, so no real solution needs to be offered.

Issue inflation: The tactic here is to intellectualize the problem. If he can distract attention from his particular issue to some related global or philosophical issue, there is no longer any particular guilt applied to himself. The issue becomes too big to be clear, so he cannot personally be in the wrong.

Detail analysis: Rather than enlarging the issue, he may narrow it. By focusing on some minor detail of the topic that really is not germane to the issue, attention can be diverted to some triviality. It is then but a step to dismissing the whole conversation as insignificant.

Oratory analysis: This dismisses the content of an argument and draws attention to your presentation of it instead. It may be flattery or criticism, but it changes the issue from a particular topic to a personal commentary. Even if we do not foolishly try to defend ourselves, often we are surprised long enough for him to redirect the conversation to something else.

There are more dramatic and obvious ones as well: biting personal remarks; physical aggression; dramatic crying; throwing a fit; or plugging his ears, screaming, and refusing to listen. Hopefully, these are clear signs of a serious problem. Do not disregard them. He is threatened by the truth you have uncovered, and you should not let that truth go just because things have become unpleasant.

The best way to handle these is to become familiar with the individual. Notice when he applies them, with whom, and how. Distance yourself from the situation enough to be able to judge it more objectively. This *is* tremendously difficult because it all sounds and feels so legitimate and personal. But objectivity is vital. You must rise above the tricks, seeing them as merely tricks, to disregard them. Firmly but respectfully press the real issue, ignoring the distractions and drama to focus on finding the truth.

If pressing the truth actually works and real issues are addressed frankly, then you are indeed lucky. If instead, there is still a drive to master the situation, he will either completely dismiss you or resort to other tricks. Examples of dismissals include: stout denial, delegating finding a solution to someone else ("passing the buck"), claiming innocence or ignorance, shallow excuses, lip service, selective hearing, or simply ignoring the speaker. While not strictly manipulative tactics themselves, they do reveal the attitude: he does not intend to engage the issue. Your fight isn't nearly over.

Distortion

The second tactic manipulators use to introduce confusion is by distorting reality. If you cannot be persuaded to look another way and to stop asking the disturbing questions, you will be served mixed truths. Outright lies are too easy to spot and perhaps too much for even the manipulator's conscience. Reason and some truth must be mixed in to produce logical explanations for some of the uncomfortable facts. He must persuade you that what you are seeing is not what you think it is. Since your awareness is awakened, your reasoning needs to be adjusted instead.

Distortions can come in several ways. There are the more overt forms, where actual evidence or testimony is tampered with to change appearances. These are often criminal, or at least more clearly deceitful, and can generally be debunked through the usual investigative processes. So manipulators tend to keep their distortions on the psychological level. When the tampering is confined to the mind, there is no paper trail to uncover. Alas, we must resort to beating an illusionist at his own game.

Distortions are difficult to unmask. They often sound true and feel right, especially if you are not accustomed to this sort of battle. They are presented with sincerity and conviction. The reasoning may seem sound. There are strong reasons to believe him. Somehow, he holds our trust, or at least our respect, enough to sway our thoughts. The credibility or the authority seems genuine, and certainly those are generally wise grounds for being convinced. But with distortions, there are other motivations working beneath the surface. Revealing truth is not his objective. Misleading you is.

Establishing Credibility

For long-term distortions to work, the manipulator's credibility must be high. Truth, however, is the enemy, so he needs to apply other methods to establish a believable story. A skilled manipulator knows very well what people want to hear so that they will trust him. He will present his story with boldness and confidence—even incorporating hints of humility, pathos, carefully chosen facts, gifts, proofs of his devotion, or a feigned interest in you to lure you in. The easy confidence appears sincere, so we believe. Surprisingly, people are not terribly logical, and credibility is often established on some very unreasonable grounds. We are only too quick to believe a person with whom we have emotional bonds, who has social sways, or who can deliver a heady argument. Then *voila!* There is credibility without truth.

Though time-consuming to establish, emotional attachment is a powerful tool. If the manipulator can get you to feel comfortable, accepted, understood, important, special, or worthy, there is a higher chance that you will easily accept whatever it is that he has to tell you. If he is familiar or charming, his arguments are usually easily accepted. Often this will go to the extent of excusing solid evidence, testimonies of witnesses, and even your own nagging doubts. This loyalty can be incredibly powerful, particularly in those individuals who have never been made to feel very worthy before. We may want to be valued so much that we are willing to endure unreasonable treatment, even at the expense of our own dignity.

The key to drawing someone into emotional attachment is by being generous: with gifts, with words, with attention, with hospitality. It is warming, and it is welcoming. His motivation is represented as noble, selfless, and ideal, and people are happy to accommodate such obvious goodness. But for a manipulator, there is never really any actual sacrifice. There might be lots of magnanimous talk, promises, and gifts at the expense of others (which may seem to have come from him), but not much solid goodwill. The basis for our trust proves to be nothing more than a convincing portrayal of a good man, temporarily.

Credibility can also be established with social mechanisms. Power, success, and popularity are all compelling forces that can be used to sway opinion. Even if they do not really exist to the levels implied, they do carry weight. What other people say or think does influence the choices we make. And to some extent, it should. But popular opinion and popular support are not wise grounds for trust. Distancing yourself from the statistics and the group mentality, is this individual worthy of your support? The proof is still in the pudding—is what he is upholding proving to be good indeed?

Perhaps the most difficult to unmask are the heady arguments. These are offered by people who are good at convincing others of the validity of their opinions. The logic of their arguments seems reasonable. Many times, there are facts to back up their claims, so it sounds good. But they play off your ignorance. What evidence has been discarded and how these facts came to be are rarely questioned. Even the logical validity of the arguments themselves is rarely dissected. They sound smart and confident, so we easily assume that they must have put considerable thought into their opinions. Or we might just be attracted by the intellectual prowess in joining their league. We do not have the time or inclination to dig deeper into what they are explaining, so they may be given our credibility simply because they sound smart.

Once the credibility has been won, we often relax our judgment and awareness. He is familiar and has been trusted, so it is a safer bet to trust him again. Yet once the idea has been firmly established that this man is worthy of our trust, the drawing out begins to happen. More and more is requested of us in return for his friendship. At first, it appears to be just the normal reciprocity of relationships, but in time, the disproportion is unreasonable. We may be drawn down a path we would rather not go simply by the force of our trust.

With these distortions, the key is to weigh the facts. As cold as that may sound, it is the safest means of evaluation. It is crucial that his attitude be weighed by his actions and not by his presentation. A convincing performance is not any assurance whatsoever of trustworthiness. It may just be a shell game. He may be interested in you only because you offer him some advantage. You may notice a distinct lack of his interest in other people who do not offer him such lucrative benefits (no matter how much you might undervalue yourself). Beware of these inconsistencies, or they may prove to be your undoing. If there is any doubt, weigh the fruits. Truth is played out in reality, not in rhetoric.

Character will tell. Test the man and you will find if his claims are worth trusting also.

Presumption

Establishing credibility is a long process. Though powerful, it does not offer the immediacy that is required in many situations. So other means of keeping control are necessary. Where others might resort to strong-arming the situation or engaging in a power play, manipulation would weaken its facade by doing so—especially if there is an audience. You will likely only see these glaring displays of taking authority in moments of weakness. Something more subtle is required. If he does not have the time to establish his authority, then he must presume it—a bold confidence that suggests that the manipulator has special power or knowledge that others fail to have. This then implies that he has a natural right to define the standard and to judge people accordingly. We may yield to this authority because somehow it does seem he has the right to take it. Perhaps it is presented with force or with gentleness, but always with a matter-of-fact demeanor that is difficult to refute. It assumes that there simply is no other way to look at it. In battle terms, it is taking the higher ground; with mind games, it is presumption.

Bold claims require a great deal of vigilance and presence of mind to refute, so do not be discouraged if you are drawn in by them. But you do need to learn from your mistakes. Your best safeguard is to come prepared. Be familiar with the tactics and, in particular, which ones you have noticed him using before. Try to distance yourself from being emotionally engaged and focus on being mentally alert. What is he really trying to accomplish by his claims and are they legitimate?

Tactics of Presumption

- **Oversimplifying:** This presents the problem much more simply than it actually is. Often it will omit incidences that are externally "minor" yet may have tremendous emotional significance. It presents the people involved as stereotypical rather than complex and expects them to fall into some prescribed theory of behavior.
  "Rosa Parks was being selfish by not offering her seat to someone else."

- **Excessive extrapolation:** Essentially, making a mountain out of a molehill. This assumes that some behavior is going to result in tremendous consequences or possibly holds some tremendous significance.
  "He's picking up a stick! He's going to hit me!"
  "You spanked me! That means you hate me!"

- **Blame shifting:** All too common, this points the blame to someone else. Someone else further up the chain of events was to blame for the outcome.
  "He made me so mad; he drove me to it."

- **Projection:** These accuse you of doing the very thing he is doing (and you are not). It is initially disorienting and keeps you on the defensive, making you look foolish if you turn the accusation back onto him.
  "You have absolutely no respect for other people's feelings!"

- **Ignored cause:** This refuses to consider the cause of an event, implying that there was none, so that an action appears completely unreasonable.
  "Can you believe that my parents just went and moved my curfew up two hours?!"

- **Raising the dead past:** This draws evidence from the past to justify current policy, even when the conditions have changed. It intentionally omits the fact that it is using outdated information. *"Don't trust him. He lost his job for being irresponsible." [Yes, when he was thirteen.]*

- **Stretching the truth:** Exaggeration, enough to look wronged or good but not enough to be caught in a lie. *"My wife won't let me eat fried food."*

- **Selective evidence:** This highlights certain facts, while ignoring others, to shed a false light on the situation. *"There are no vegetables on the table, so I must not have to eat any."*

- **Misdiagnosed motivation:** This blatantly assumes that a reason for a behavior is sinister or selfish. It boldly judges what it really cannot know. *"You are just determined to make me miserable."* *"Your son moved out because he can't stand you!"*

- **Vague implications:** These fail to offer any concrete evidence to leave you to judge a situation for yourself, but simply imply that the circumstances are so clear that they need no explanation. His evaluation is perfectly sufficient for you. *"If you only knew what I know, you would be appalled!"*

- **Weak analogy:** There is an analogy made between your situation and another more clear-cut one that would obviously make him the protagonist. As the analogous example clearly points in favor of him, so should this one. *"What are you, the Princess and the Pea?!"*

- **Claiming clairvoyance:** This tactic presumes to know your mind, desires, thoughts, preferences, or understanding better than you do yourself.
  "You don't believe that!"

- **Confrontational demand:** Even if not aggressively delivered, these can be disorienting. They suggest that the situation is your problem and that there is really only one choice you have—to do what he thinks you should.
  "What are you going to do about it?"

- **Redefining normal:** This claims that some offensive behavior is actually quite normal and should be accepted as such. It implies that the problem lies with you and not with the behavior.
  "Everyone insults their employees; it motivates them better."

- **Blurring the line:** This technique makes the boundary between right and wrong particularly unclear. By blending two ideas together, he is free to take the most advantageous qualities of each. It often ends by implying that his motivation was pure, so his actions (however offensive or destructive) are completely innocent.
  "It isn't stealing; it's borrowing."

The examples here illustrate the mentality, though the actual claims are immeasurably more subtle and come unexpectedly to catch you off-guard. In addition, they are personal and pointed, so they are designed to cause more pain. In the heat of the moment, it is very difficult to clearly determine not only what is happening, but also what the best strategy for unmasking the distortion would be. Even if you do have the presence of mind to address it well, things can quickly degrade. To onlookers, it will just look like a blame game. And there is not much benefit in that for anyone.

With distortion, the battle is largely in your mind. Its purpose is to get you to doubt so that you will easily accept whatever conclusion he wants to press. Even if you accept it with reluctance and not out of agreement, he has accomplished his goal: you conform. Often the effect for you, though, is only confusion. You are not entirely certain what is happening, though something may not feel quite right about it. But in the uncertainty, he can easily press harder to achieve his goals despite you. Bold decision inevitably wins out over uneasy doubt.

But bold and confident declaration is no sign of truth. If his strategy is to take the higher ground, yours needs to be to level the playing field. It is not likely you will be able to out-argue him, but that does not mean you cannot be equally bold. Ideally, you would briefly state that what he is claiming is complete rot and walk away unaffected. Even if you cannot decipher exactly what is taking place and which strategies he is using to press you into his will, you still can have the strength to dismiss it. If necessary, you can figure it out later. The important point to make is that you will not be pressed into a situation where your freedom and your dignity will be undermined. Seeing clearly enough to do this with confidence is vital to unmasking manipulation.

Introducing Ambiguity

Confusion arises when there is a lack of clarity. If you are uncertain what a word means, how to measure an attribute, the relative importance of certain facts, or any number of other things, you are at a distinct disadvantage—especially if you are up against someone who will freely claim to know such things. Even if you believe you are certain, it may take much less effort than you might imagine to transform it into uncertainty. Particularly to fair-minded individuals, it only takes a little distortion to introduce ambiguity. Only a small wrench can clog up the works. A small push toward doubt can open up enough opportunity for him to wreck havoc. And control feeds off of this chaos.

Because the tactics are so subtle, you need to be aware of the possible techniques before you are up against them.

Tactics that Create Ambiguity

• **Ambiguity of the relationship:** This is the overarching deception of manipulation. Confusion over the exact nature of the relationship drives the control. Though he talks like an ally, when he feels a threat, he proves to be no friend at all. Often you are not simply abandoned but exploited—but always furtively and just infrequently enough to be completely destabilizing to you—while maintaining his innocent facade.

The same ploy may be applied more directly. Business relations are of a different nature than personal ones. Contacts, associates, and acquaintances are different than friends. Where cooperation on one level may be understood, cooperation on another level does not necessarily follow.

> *Lucas is running the campaign for Lyle, who wants to win the county commissioner election. Lucas volunteers large amounts of his time to the cause so is happy to orchestrate the printing and distribution of extra stickers—until he is left paying the tab himself. Lyle argues that Lucas needs to put his money where his mouth is and he's not asking any more of him than from his other contributors, so he should not need to be reimbursed.*

Good personal relationships do not rely on pressure. Demanding one's rights undermines the privileges of a friend. Shifting the expectations of a relationship suddenly is neither respectful nor reasonable. Trying to help himself to the best of both associations is double-dipping and completely maddening. Draw a firm line quickly.

- **Percentage ambiguity:** How often something occurs matters. If someone yells at you once, there could be any number of understandable reasons for it. If someone yells at you daily, there are entirely different workings afoot. Manipulation plays into this game by sliding the scale. If he can change the perception of the duration and frequency of incidences, the understood motivations behind them are shifted. He may make it sound like an incident is rare or regular, depending on which is to his advantage. He may imply that you are petty—that you are making a major issue out of something that is uncommon—or perverted—that what was an isolated mistake on your part is actually a chronic problem. This tactic creates a point of doubt that is easily built upon and exasperating to discredit.

Anna gets straight As on her report cards, and her teachers report that she is a very conscientious student. Yet anytime she gets less than a perfect score on an assignment, her mother harshly quizzes her about each of her mistakes. When Mom discusses the matter with her friends, though, she implies that Anna has a tendency to become lax and sloppy, and so she occasionally needs to firmly press her back on track. The fellow mothers nod in sympathy; they each have a child who needs an extra push to achieve more.

- **Ambiguity of meaning:** This is essentially a word game. One particular word may suggest something quite different than another of its synonyms. For example, "disgusting" has a stronger connotation than "unpleasant." By furtively inserting such exaggerations into his argument, technically what he is saying might be true, but the implications drawn have been decidedly rigged. Other subtle distortions, such as an inaccurate pronoun choice, can lead to undeserved guilt or honor. You may be tempted to bicker over word choice, but that is exactly all it will appear to be: bickering. He is not likely to back down from his carefully planned deception, so you really can hope to accomplish nothing by arguing. Silent protest probably carries more weight than any other option at that moment.

The opposite tactic that introduces an ambiguity of language is bringing into question the technical meanings of the words. By dissecting your particular word choice, he may discredit your stance. (e.g. *"What do you mean I did when you said I yelled at you? Explain what you mean by yelling."*) It suggests that because one word is not precisely accurate, then your whole line of persuasion is likewise flawed. If it does nothing else, this will certainly sidetrack the real issue. For you, it is important to hold to your choices, even if they were slightly arbitrary. Stick to the main point. Any hint of hesitation will feed the doubts he has already raised. Sort it out in your own mind later; for now, be unmoved. The more you engage in futile explanations, the more foolish you will appear.

Other methods, identified more as logical fallacies, include changing the meaning of a word in the middle of an argument, intentionally using vague language, changing the way a phrase is said to imply something other than the words spoken (e.g. sarcasm or selected word emphasis), quoting out of context, and repetition or rephrasing to imply deeper significance or conviction. The subtle nature of these tactics can be very disconcerting. They are often applied seamlessly and certainly without warning. But regardless of whether you can specifically identify the methodology at the time, often your gut will warn you of foul play. It is best to just drop the conversation. Bowing out need not imply defeat, but that you are disgusted with the games.

• **Shifting cause and effect:** Much of discerning sources of problems lies in understanding cause and effect. If there is a negative result, we look for a cause to prevent a repetition of the incident. If it is to the advantage of the manipulator to confuse this source (likely to avoid detection), the relation between the cause and the effect is blurred. Either a spurious cause is suggested, it is implied that there was no cause (the event was random or inevitable), or the cause and effect are reversed. While hardly conceivable in a laboratory, this latter technique is particularly effective with emotional or relational situations.

> *Clare has concluded that it is not worth arguing with Thomas when he is angry because he screams and is unreasonable. She has learned to wait until he cools off before discussing issues. When the next heated argument arises, Clare slowly fades out of the discussion. This enrages Thomas more and his accusations intensify. She calmly requests he stop shouting, whereupon he claims, "I'm yelling because you won't talk to me."*

In this situation, it is best to distance yourself from the accusations and their implications. Try to view the situation as objectively as possible, despite the nasty personal remarks. Though it may not be helpful to share your conclusions with the arguer (it may just open up more clouding of the truth), you must be convinced in your own mind enough to dismiss the claims as completely unfair. Judge the evidence for yourself and then rest on what you know.

- **Shifting perspective:** Often we are not completely conscious of how we make judgments and draw conclusions. If they are objective, introducing a subjective perspective can cause us to reconsider the facts. Maybe emotional or relational dynamics should be taken into consideration. If your judgment is largely subjective, introducing cold facts may discredit your conclusion. Maybe the objective stand is more solid. Either way, doubts are introduced. Manipulation delights in prying up your certainty, especially if it poses a threat to his control. So by taking the opposite perspective of the issue, regardless of its true significance, he may cause you to pause, weakening your case.

Michael is looking into joining one of the freshman fall sport teams. He mentions football, and his father objects, "The rate of injury in young players is excessively high, and the time commitment is heavy. There are better sports for serious scholars that can be just as enjoyable." So Michael suggests he might like golf. His father then argues that golf is really not a sport, and there is a certain elitist attitude that the members of a golf team have. He certainly does not want his son to become a snob. Soccer is his father's strong recommendation, despite Michael's expressed dislike for it.

• **Ambiguity of degree:** Degree measures magnitude. However, when the scale is subjective (e.g. one person's extreme pain may be equivalent to another's tolerable ache), there is plenty of room for ambiguity—either exaggeration or minimization. These generally involve emotional issues, which have no objective measurement. A person can be angry from just a flare-up over a minor incident or furious over extended injustice. A scream may arise from anywhere between a harmless spider to an imminent threat. An opinion may be merely a random thought or a solid conclusion based on extended study. A preference may be shown based on unwavering devotion or simply a lack of any good option. A request may be made because of an urgent need or a whimsical want. The interpretation of the degree of importance is vital to judging its true significance.

Though it may be used to deceive you, more often this method will be used to discredit you to others. By suggesting that your judgment of this degree of importance is skewed—either hyper-sensitive toward minor issues or overly indifferent toward substantial good—you can quickly be significantly discredited. Your interpretation of the facts will be minimized while his are glorified. Regardless of how much evidence you may present to support your stand, a suspicion of your reasoning ability has been introduced. Your judgment has been undermined, the value of your voice and contributions have been cheapened, and you will have a great deal of difficulty regaining your credibility. A silent and steady demonstration of good judgment, contrary to report, is your strongest hope.

Dustin is dressing for an important business dinner. His wife Elise, recovering from a serious but discreet surgery, is doing her best to be present and presentable; but Dustin is being excessively exacting. When they arrive at the dinner, Dustin is annoyed with her because her slip is showing and says so rather too loudly. As bravely as she has been trying to bear up under all the pain and tension, Elise tears up and excuses herself. Dustin comments to his coworkers, "She can be so touchy!" For the rest of the evening, Elise must endure artificial sweetness and conciliatory stories about minor embarrassments, without being in a position to explain herself fairly at all.

• **Ambiguity of significance:** Generally, the relative importance of choices, actions, and words are very vague. Judging them in a particular culture is a skill developed from experience and observation. There are no rules for determining the significance of, say, a slight shrug; it depends on the dynamics of the situation, the individual, and the timing. With mature people, we expect fair use and judgment of these things; most of us have a good sense of when a slight shrug has significance and when it does not. But in the manipulation game, this is an open invitation to bend rules that are not clear. There is plenty of room to foster doubt. He may intentionally misinterpret those signals from others. Or he may lead you astray with implications made by his gestures, facial expressions, intonation, unfinished sentences, omitted facts, or other tricks that are technically not lies. It just leads you to believe something that is not completely true.

A manipulator will effortlessly slide the scale: a significant fact can be transformed into an insignificant detail; an act of goodness may be tainted with evil intent; a gesture of disgust can be exaggerated into a harsh verbal insult; a wishful possibility can be extrapolated into a hard promise; a mere theory can be inflated into solid fact—or vice versa, whichever is to his advantage. After all, it is all a game of shifting the viewpoint. Easy dismissal and confident presentation can carry his points far, while you are still trying to figure out exactly what happened. And if you are having trouble figuring it out, it is far less likely that any observers will see through the illusions, either. Even if he is pressed, he may consent to slide the scale back a little, but really his purpose has already been achieved—to unsettle you.

If possible, a calm presentation of your side of the story is vital. Generally, people are willing to be open-minded when they are presented both sides. The trick, however, comes when you are somehow unable to do so; perhaps you are in a socially awkward position or not even present. Confronting the offender is important, but if you are caught in manipulation, it likely will produce little effect. You may have to just discredit all implications by the long and tireless demonstration of your own strength of character. Make the extreme claims unbelievable.

- **Shifting standards:** Probably the clearest violations of integrity of them all, shifting standards can be maddening. You may believe you understand what the expectations are, and then when you have nearly reached them, suddenly there is a higher or different standard. Not only is your effort often wasted but your hope also is dashed. It is like trying to keep your balance on shifting sand—it is exhausting work with little progress to show for it.

The specific methods of shifting standards are more easily identified than most other tricks, largely because the surest sign is that this new declaration throws you completely off-balance. What you thought was suddenly is not. Certainly, life brings unexpected turns of events, and we do need to have a certain degree of flexibility to deal with new expectations. But with the regularity and indifference of manipulation, there is an expectation not that you be just flexible but fluid. You must instantly conform to the new requirements. These may be broad, as in abruptly pressing you into adopting a new roll in a relationship or job. Or they may be more particular: holding a double standard, offering unfair comparisons, continually raising the bar, judging you by hindsight, presenting incomplete facts, splitting hairs. There is something not quite honest about it all. You find that an objective standard is illusive, mostly likely because there is none.

> *Carlton gets very annoyed when people ride his tail on the road. He vehemently insists that they are creating an unnecessarily dangerous situation and that they are violating the safe distance principle. But when Carlton is in a hurry and behind a vehicle that he considers is going too slowly, they are suddenly nonchalant drivers who are completely indifferent to other people's responsibilities and in need of a little motivation. So he rides their tail.*

These types of distortions are largely hypocritical in nature—you will find the tricks he habitually plays become intolerable when there is even a chance that they are being played on him. And then they return to being acceptable and normal when he is their source. So the behavior must be addressed. A sweeping accusation will be poorly received, so the behaviors need to be dismantled one-by-one. By confronting the specific hypocrisy of the individual actions, there is greater potency—he must justify himself. Whatever he has to offer will be weak, so do not be dissuaded. He needs to face the power of an objective standard.

These persuasive pushes are powerful because at times, they *are* fair points. Sometimes these tactics have validity and do carry a strong argument. They are sometimes reasonable. But in the midst of manipulation, the purpose behind the words is not good. The subtleties are meant to deceive. It is easy to be drawn in, so be on your guard. If things begin to feel normal, do not simply accept it—look deeper first.

Division

Possibly the most basic of offensive war strategies is to divide and conquer. If a wedge can be driven into the opposition's defense, then they are significantly weakened. Either a division between the troops and their supplies or a splitting of the forces will introduce a tremendous weakness. This simple principle has won and lost dozens of battles, and it applies just as effectively to mental war.

Manipulation thrives on your weaknesses. The more division they can create within your own mind, the less pressure is needed to get you to move and the more easily he can master your decisions. It is disturbing if you are aware of what is happening, but you rarely are. Stealth is their key. So beware of people using these strategies:

Isolating

The most effective means of dividing is to isolate. Isolation attempts to remove other perspectives, choices, and opinions from the table. Then you can easily be mastered because the opposition has been eliminated or at least greatly reduced. This opposition would be the people who have a genuine concern for you or who offer a more well-rounded perspective than your manipulator does. If he can isolate you, then he can redefine what is normal and press you into whatever his design for you is. Often this happens gradually, so it is not so noticeable. Certainly, loyalty in one area requires us to sever ties to some degree in other areas. In this gradual drawing away, it is impossible to notice when you have crossed the line to being, in essence, cut off. Even if there are some loose ties to the outside world, the significant decisions inevitably fall to the manipulator's interests. This is when you have become trapped.

The following is a list of common isolation tactics, though a combination of them is more often employed:

- **Physical distance:** You are not with other people very often. When you are, they are people of a very limited variety. Those who would actually be interested in investing into you personally are purposefully kept far away. Somehow the circumstances are arranged to make it very difficult for you to get to other people, especially those who love you the most.

- **Overburdening:** This technique simply loads you down with too many responsibilities. Your contributions to the cause are too important for you to leave them. Your personal needs are trivialized for the sake of other, "higher," purposes.

- **Fear:** Somehow the outside world is presented as too dangerous or too difficult to be considered as a place to go. The hazards are too extreme, so your isolation is disguised as a protective measure.

- **Purity:** The outside world, rather than being dangerous, is perverted. The corruption or temptation is too rampant and deceptive, so your isolation is a moral stand against its depravity.

- **Inferiority:** This plays off of your own insecurity (made worse by continual manipulation). It implies that you are really in no condition to face society. Somehow you are too weak to face the harsh reality of the real world. No one else would have or value you. Your manipulator does, though, so you ought to stay where you are.

- **Superiority:** This suggests that you are great because of your association with the manipulator's power structure. Leaving, or even trying to view the situation outside of his perspective, is a sign of intolerable weakness. If you want to be strong and right, you will stay put.

Isolation can be very damaging because it is so thoroughly effective. No matter how much you might justify and excuse the isolation for the sake of "the cause," you are still disconnected. Your social dimension is starved, and that will inevitably lead to damage. But isolation is also the clearest sign to outsiders (especially those who love you) that there is a serious problem. They may respect your choices and leave you alone, but likely there lingers an ache inside of them that you have been trapped. Recognize this, because you will need them for support.

Keeping Things on Edge

It is to a manipulator's advantage to keep things on edge. If those who are working for him are kept tottering between survival and disaster, they will cling to he who holds the rope. The manipulator wants to be the one holding the rope. A man of weak character can easily master others if he keeps them at risk. It may look like he is helping because he is in the role of the rescuer, but there is no genuine rescue. He is only guarding his strength by freely spending theirs.

Keeping you on edge usually involves limiting something you need: resources, time, help, rest, sympathy, understanding, perspective, dignity, something. It may be in the form of a tight budget, high demands, urgency, inattention, or a host of other pressures—spoken or unspoken, real or exaggerated. But somehow any margin in your life is filled with his demands. You have no leeway, no room for mistakes, no mercy. At times, of course, things are tight, but chronic tightness has deeper causes. They cannot continue indefinitely.

A common technique for doing this is by exaggerating his own weakness or principles. Pity or even functionality can demand that you fill in the gaps for his inabilities, often stretching you far beyond what you should bear. Here is a list of common reputations that disguise control and keep you stretched thin:

- **Poverty or stinginess**: He looks poor. This has the added advantage in that it stirs up pity in others, who may then be willing to give to "help." This gives him leverage over them also. Meanwhile, money is being discreetly siphoned off for his pet projects or to protect his control.

- **Suffering:** He looks like he is suffering miserably. It could be physical suffering. Illness and disability stir pity. It could be mental suffering. Social or work pressures, emotional pain, depression, and past hurts can weigh heavily on a human spirit. Only he takes no steps toward genuine healing but only milks the situation...

- **Moral Weakness:** He looks like he is struggling to overcome a burden. Bad behaviors are rampant, and there are a number of roots of these flaws: difficult childhood, family problems, economic hardship, personal failures, hormonal imbalance. It is a type of suffering that can stir pity. Except if it is about control, he will not bother to improve.

- **Fear:** He looks like he is afraid and needs reassurance, often requiring you to erect huge "safety nets." Control disguised by fear will often spur you to invest where he does not. You may find that his fear mysteriously fades without your support.

- **Dedication to a Cause:** It seems like he is trying hard to live up to a high standard that he has for himself. But if it is disguising the suppression of others, there is a severe flaw in the cause. No matter how noble the goal, it should never interfere with the freedom and dignity of the innocent. Question what the true motivation is.

- **A Higher Calling:** Externally, he looks holy and claims that he has the authority of God behind him. But the lack of genuine goodness is evidence enough of his artificiality. Beware of charlatans. Piety can be an excuse for committing all sorts of indignities. How many heinous crimes have been committed in the name of God! If the means to the end are ugly, the end will most certainly also be ugly.

These are similar to the strategy of a professional con artist. He wants you to believe that he is something less than he really is so that he will gain your trust and investment. His real goal, though, is only to deplete you of your resources. Do not be drawn in by the act.

The key to overcoming this tactic is catching your breath long enough to recognize what is happening. Once there is an awakening to the situation, generally there is some means available for creating margin. Refusing to cooperate or contribute is a good starting point. Your sanity, in the form of rest and refreshment, is important. However heavy outside obligations may seem, regaining your strength should not be neglected. Bring in professionals instead to help address his concerns. This also gives you time to assess. Strategically, it is more efficient in every way to your productivity. It opens a door of opportunity for you to think more clearly, which controls fear.

Picking a Fight

Stirring up anger is an easy method of creating chaos. If it is starting an argument between yourself and someone else, the purpose is to create division. By drawing attention to a difference in opinion, a natural distrust is aroused. Someone who might serve to strengthen your cause is shown to be less than ideal. If you do not find this significant, your manipulator will. He is likely to use it to try to alienate you from that individual later.

If the argument is between the two of you, then the purpose is different. Rarely is the issue at hand the real issue. He is not looking to settle a disagreement but to win, and likely win more than just the argument. If he is determined to dominate, controversies are for introducing distortion or doubt. Somehow by arguing, he gets an advantage—perhaps socially, emotionally, or intellectually. He is master. You are portrayed as inferior, and likely you walk away feeling that way, too. He wants to shake your confidence in your own judgment and abilities. You have probably never gained anything from heated arguments with him. Maybe you are fully aware of this. But he knows how to push your buttons just to draw you into the fray and make you feel foolish or defeated. Aggravating but not unmanageable, if you are on your toes.

The best strategy is to avoid arguments. They are not about

expressing a perspective and finding resolution anyway. With manipulation, the purpose is strictly to undermine your strength. Calmly dismiss them with as much presence of mind as possible and move on. They are created to unsteady you, and you will always walk away the loser. So it is best to walk away before you become the loser. Not easily done because his point may sound reasonable and fair, but know that this game is played according to his rules. Whatever is tempting you to join in the debate is probably not worth it. If the issue is genuine, address it calmly later, focusing on the facts. For now, play it safe. Calmly dismiss them with as much presence of mind as possible and move on.

Creating Moral Dilemmas

There is a wide range of intangible things we value, such as peace, safety, and reputation. Largely, these are universally valued, and reasonable people respect this and unconsciously hold by their standards. There is a sympathy when you are torn between family obligations and work responsibilities. Others usually understand, mostly because they have been there before. There is a willingness to extend not only mercy but also goodwill in helping you to maneuver the difficulties.

Not so with manipulators. This vulnerability is an opportunity for exploitation to them. They may not only leave you to wallow in your moral dilemmas but also create them. If they can put or keep you in a vulnerable situation, they have more power to sway it to their advantage. You looking and feeling like a fool automatically gives them more power; they are superior for not having such problems.

The key to creating moral dilemmas is to get ideals you value to be in opposition. These are often intangible things that cannot be measured, so there is no real objective means of making a decision. Health, duty, stability, loyalty, and love are all good things that are difficult to choose between. You must trust in your own judgments and experience. How hesitant you are in making these calls is directly related to how vulnerable you are to a manipulator's tricks. If you are stumped, he has an open invitation to press his own agenda. Watch out!

> *Jason, age seventeen, has a grandmother, Stella, who regularly goes to watch his baseball games. Every time Jason goes up to bat, Stella yells in her booming voice, "Blow me a kiss, dear." If he fails to do this, she will loudly complain at length to those sitting nearby how she has been unjustly scorned—certainly disturbing Jason at bat as well as his parents and the other onlookers. He knows, though, by blowing her a kiss, he is playing into her control. It would definitely cost him a piece of his own self-respect, if not the respect of his teammates. But even a friendly wave instead has failed to satisfy her.*

Moral dilemmas drive confusion. The choices are there, and both look bad. This can throw us off balance and can cause us to doubt ourselves, even briefly. This momentary weakness is exactly what a manipulator can exploit. He will strike when your guard is down. In addition, he can use them to highlight your shame. Whatever you choose will reflect on you badly somehow. So this too gives reason to pause. Your shame is his power.

Dismantling this trick always involves a risk. You will have to take a firm stand on one side or the other and stick to it at all costs. Really, the bigger issue at stake is your freedom and not the moral dilemma at all. Likely whatever choice you make will work out. Your freedom is the more significant prize at stake. If you battle to regain your independence first, you may find that most of your moral dilemmas dissolve, because they are not useful for controlling you any longer.

Staunch Irresponsibility

In a partnership, there are some expectations of working together. There is an unspoken understanding that all parties will do their best to reach a common goal, each part contributing to help the others. Staunch irresponsibility undermines this process. Either by emphatically refusing to rise up to the need or by "proving" himself to be incompetent (break-the-dishes-so-you-won't-have-to-wash-them-anymore ploy), a manipulator will drop his load onto you. It is not difficult to make life difficult if you are willing to be difficult.

Candace has been looking forward to going out with her friends ever since the baby was born four months ago. Her husband, Sam, has been encouraging her to do it and promised to babysit for the duration of the theater performance. Shortly before she is to leave, Candace briefs him on the diaper changing and bedtime routines. Sam stares at her incredulously and claims, "I'm not doing all that. He'll be fine in the crib." Her hurried arguments that an infant needs more attention than that fall on deaf ears. Candace has no time to find a sitter, so she chooses instead to stay at home.

To the manipulator, the goal is control. Regardless of how much of your trust it has cost him, he has gotten you to do exactly what he intended you to do. It drives a wedge between you and some source of your strength. You are helpless, and while you both may know it, it is difficult to know what to do to get out of it, especially if the suffering of others is at stake. For conscientious individuals, though, the choice is easy: sacrifice yourself for the sake of the greater good. What rest you might otherwise have enjoyed will not be refreshing if you are concerned about the welfare of others. In addition, the chaos that you will find left for you afterward will more than destroy any restoration you managed to obtain. If you have lived with this for any length of time, you find that it is not even worth it. You may just automatically take the long and tedious road around his obstinacy. Possibly a good temporary solution, but it still leaves you carrying the entire load yourself.

This is where you will need to be shrewd. You will have to rise up to demand responsibility. He must be denied his creature comforts if you are being denied your peace. Unfortunately, this will often require you to suffer along with him in the lack, but you know that it is for a far greater good in the end. Key in on what he values and cease to provide that service for him. It may appear phenomenally selfish or irresponsible, but if you are dealing with the behavior of a two-year-old, you will have to treat him like a two-year-old.

> Hal is upset about the household expenses, which his wife, Sarah, handles. Though she is very frugal, Hal accuses Sarah of spending entirely too much on groceries. Meanwhile, he has been liberally spending to expand his motorcycle collection. Sarah is disgusted. She doesn't know how to reduce the household expenses any further. So she declares that she is turning the shopping over to Hal; it is no longer her responsibility. Hal is furious, so he refuses to buy groceries, either. Their meals then become interesting: stale crackers, baked beans, and parched corn.

Erecting firm boundaries with consequences is vital. Though losing control drives him to create more chaos, physical discomfort does carry a strong point. If you are dealing with a battle of the wills, then engage in the battle. He wants domination, you want equality. Fight for the justice of your cause. Though his determination may be strong and he is highly skilled at a variety of tricks, your character is stronger, and that is a tremendous advantage. As crazy as it may feel, it is not madness but desperation. Act with calculation to make it count.

You need to be focused, clear-headed, and strong. The battle against provoked confusion is intense. Manipulators will strike with focus, urgency, and intensity. While your mind is uncertain, manipulation plays on your emotions to draw you into a bondage. In every sense, this should not be—but it is. So you must be certain that you are committed to standing by the truth. Despite the temptation to just end the battle, you are the one who must see it through. There will be strong opposition, and often the odds will not appear to be in your favor. But if you are too patient with deceit, it will find its talking point (again). The more intense the battle, the more extreme measures you will have to take. It *is* bad. And the more you feel it, the more you need to understand; the more you understand it, the more you need to fight it.

The goal of all these tricks is for you to become absorbed into his agendas. You must not be your own master. If you are divided, you are weak. If you are isolated, you are helpless. An undecided thinker is easily led. But even better, a thinker already under his influence does not need to be led. In the midst of the onslaught of low and dirty mind games, you may be tempted to give up. It may seem that tepid success is hardly worth the fight. Beware, though, because the victim mentality offers no better life under the thumb of manipulation.

5
THE VICTIM MENTALITY TRAP

AFTER EXTENDED EXPOSURE to abuse, in this case manipulation, victims must shift their mindsets in order to cope with the flood of injustice. Being repeatedly hurt and being helpless to relieve or escape it requires the mind to adjust to a new normal—a new set of expectations. If you expect that a blow to the stomach is coming, you might not be able to stop it, but you can at least brace yourself for it so that it does not do so much damage. We do the same for emotional blows. If we expect to be treated with disrespect, indignity, and injustice, we will not be caught off guard when they come. "Rolling with the punches" is a well-known boxing strategy. Taking the blows head-on without anticipating them will only leave you the seriously injured loser.

So victims shift their expectations. Instead of expecting to be treated with respect, we expect to be treated with contempt and disdain. We expect to be dismissed, disregarded, disbelieved. We anticipate that our voices will not be heard, our opinions will not matter, our dreams will be treated as foolish, our needs counted as petty. Though we hate it and might resist in spirit, mentally we resign ourselves to being shamed, used, judged, blamed, and mistreated. It is how we can survive.

When the blows keep coming relentlessly and there is little to counteract their poison, slowly, slowly our wills and spirits are broken. We sacrifice pieces of our dignity just to keep surviving. We may find ourselves helpless but not yet hopeless. There is still some fight left, some determination to find a way out. The desperation leads to desperate measures—all sorts of avenues may be explored, any sort of advice tested. We hold onto our will to fight this because we know instinctively that there is something wrong. In our weakness, though, we find we are fighting a very formidable opponent. He is shameless, bold, strong, and full of a whole bag of tricks. It is an easy matter to him to discredit our feeble and desperate efforts. Eventually our options are exhausted and our strength is spent. When all has failed, helplessness gives way to hopelessness. If you have concluded that you could not or should not be rescued, welcome to the victim mentality.

Instead of just expecting to be treated with injustice, the victim mentality also accepts it. It ushers the mind into a whole new way of thinking. Largely instead of problem solving, life becomes problem ingestion. The challenge is not how to employ resources to change situations but how to change yourself so that you can keep bearing the blows the problems bring. Outwardly, there may appear to be little change at first. The garbage is still out of public sight, and you are still going through the motions of living. But inwardly, it is accumulating inside of you instead of being dealt with properly. Your emotional waste disposal facility operates in overdrive, and there is no energy left for anything else.

Climbing Out of the Pit

There are three obstacles to getting out of the victim mentality: yourself, your manipulator, and bystanders. Likely, at some point, you have been aware of these, and the sheer impossibility of tackling them all is what may have kept you from action earlier. Frankly, they will still be there no matter how long you wait. As impossible as it may seem, they must be understood and faced.

There is some value in understanding the obstacles that you may be creating for yourself. Often these are understandable responses to the overwhelming situation, but they are still obstacles. Rationalizations, fears, misunderstandings, and coping mechanisms all play into a victim identity. They need to be addressed systematically so that you can find the strength to fight for justice, a justice that extends far beyond yourself.

Dissolving Your Own Rationalizations

Rationalizations give reasons for staying where you are. In the confusion of manipulation, these can become quite elaborate. Good judgment is blurred by entangled devotions, extreme pain, despair, and fear. In some sense, you may have even absorbed the thoughts and reasoning of your oppressor, just to avoid inciting his anger. Your sense of good may have become so dulled that you cannot imagine true happiness. Though you must identify your own rationalizations yourself, the following are a few examples:

- *I haven't given him enough of a chance. Once he realizes what he is doing, things will get better. He just needs a chance to notice.*
- *I deserve this. Somehow I have made a terrible mistake in my life, and these are the consequences. Maybe someday I will understand how the punishment is just.*
  I have so little worth that this is just the best I can expect.
- *Enduring is a sign of great strength. I am strong enough to bear these blows. I will not cave into the weakness of retaliation.*
- *It is my duty. I must remain loyal to my cause, my religious piety, or my family tradition. The self-sacrifice is noble, the suffering is purifying, and the promise for a future reward is big, so I must endure.*
- *No one believes in me, so I must be the one who is wrong. No*

one else sees the problem at all, so it must be all in my head. I must deal with it there.

- **Relief is enough.** *Life is neither fair nor easy. Some patches of relief are as good as it gets. This is the best I can expect. I must make it work.*
- **My life is a lesson to others.** *At least I am an example of what others should not do. Maybe my life can be their warning.*
- **If it were not me, it would be someone else.** *Somebody is going to end up suffering for this. Since I'm here already, I'm best suited to bear it. At least it is sparing another innocent soul.*
- **Certain misery is better than complete uncertainty.** *This is all I know and where I have invested everything. I would have to give up my identity, my purpose, and my survival skills. An escape would just leave me floundering, which doesn't look like an improvement.*

What all of these rationalizations do is leave you alone to keep being harmed, without spurring you on to offer any resistance. They scream for you to stay victimized. No one deserves to be stripped of his dignity without having committed a clear and severe offense. Errors in thinking, oversights, misguided judgments, and blind choices are not at all grounds for indefinite bondage without hope of redemption. Endurance is strength, but sometimes it is time to use that strength to fight instead. Where there is a complete lack of inherent good, where the effort invested is not producing obvious improvement, perhaps it is not worth your effort. Rise up to be a positive example, something that will inspire others to a brighter hope. Greater good can come from boldly establishing right than from endlessly enduring wrong. You must battle to overcome these obstacles in your own mind firmly first, because there will come similar ones from the outside soon enough. You must be confident enough to answer your own doubts before you can boldly counter another who is determined to corner you with them later.

Coping Mechanisms and Their Pitfalls

Surviving in the midst of the situation, and even through the stages of recovery, is of course vital. We must have a means of managing. Coping mechanisms are what we employ when our efforts at real solutions have failed. They are a means of survival, what can keep us going just a little longer until something more significant can be accomplished. They are often tried and true strategies for helping us endure when there seems no other option. They keep us alive until the troops can come through.

The following are five common ethical coping mechanisms that people under manipulation employ. Manipulation is often a very subtle beast, though, so even identifying what is happening is a tremendous feat. Coping is a wise first step, but only until the problem is clearly identified. Like all such strategies, over a long period of time, there are significant drawbacks to them. The coping methods can themselves become obstacles.

Appeasement

For strong opinions strongly expressed, there are generally two reactions: a counterattack or appeasement. Trying to calm or satisfy a person who has an intense focus is a logical place to start. Certainly, there must have been some trigger that caused his alarm, and the humane thing to do is to try to address the problem. In normal interactions, this is certainly the thoughtful response. Once the urgency has been reduced by appeasing it, there is greater peace to see clearly and make more objective decisions. So appeasement is meant to restore some peace so that things can get back in order.

This method fails, however, when the motivation behind the drama is control. What was meant as an act of charity can become a way of life. If strong reactions and inappropriate behavior are a means of getting what he wants, a manipulator may begin to use them indiscriminately. Anger, throwing a fit, making a scene—rather than real expressions of pain—may be just a means to an end: getting his way. His bad behavior gets good results. If he acts angry, the reaction is extra attention and effort. If he pressures, he is given special favors. If there is dissatisfaction, people change to accommodate him. He learns from your efforts that he can easily get what he wants by being unpleasant. But what is it costing you?

This approach begins to cost you everything in return for nothing. Trying to appease control can stir his appetite for more, and you are drawn into endless giving. The original condition may have seemed minor, so you act out of mercy. Then suddenly it is not good enough—not because you did not satisfy the demand, but because you are still free. So the conditions are tightened. The more calisthenics you perform to find a way to compromise, the more you find the demands increase.

> *Mr. Holbrook is the new office manager of personnel in an open floor plan. The employees, used to open communication, freely speak to each other across the room. Mr. Holbrook finds this intolerable and establishes a low volume policy. The flexible employees reluctantly oblige, but Mr. Holbrook is still displeased. Soon background music is banned, then talking altogether, then listening to music on headphones, then non-business interoffice texts. The employees resort to giving each other signals behind his back, but they all fully expect to be reprimanded for this at any moment.*

By continuing to tolerate it, eventually it can become impossible to be yourself. If you find this is the case, it really was not about the original condition at all; it is not merely some pet-peeve you ought to humor. It is about control.

Being used might not seem like it matters to anyone else besides you. You may not like it, but maybe you endure it to keep the peace. You may reason that it does no harm and may even be preventing harm to others. But if you are feeding into the power and control by appeasing, you are doing far more harm than good, however unintentionally. Your fear is fueling the tyranny, as insignificant as your contribution might seem to be. Even unwillingly, you are support, and support fuels power.

Whatever the motivation for appeasement, it has another pitfall besides extending the misery. It feeds the illusion of normalcy. People will take your superhuman tolerance to mean the problem is not serious. They will assume that your investment into the relationship is your free choice, because it appears that you are giving without compulsion. You give to prevent a disaster that you are certain will come, but they never see. All that you are sacrificing to keep the peace is covering up the evidence of the real problem and its real source. Not only are you getting yourself deeper into a dark hole, you are perpetuating the lie that things are fine.

Distancing

The easiest of all strategies is to just stay away. The less available you make yourself, the less a manipulator can take advantage of you. Alas, though, this is not always feasible. But the mechanism still has value. Avoidance comes in the form of creating havens—sacred places where the manipulator is not likely to come. It is here that you must find some peace, enjoy your dignity, and restore your strength for the next round of blows. Like anyone enduring long periods of duress, you must thoroughly relax between the encounters. Wasting your strength in anxious anticipation of the pain only leaves you weaker for the hard blows when they inevitably come. You must embrace health when you can.

When physical distancing is not possible, emotional distancing will have to do. Essentially, you just withdrawn your sympathy. Though you may defer to his wishes (keep your nose down, your mouth shut, and do your duty), there is no devotion. Nor should there be if you have no voice. Though some other bond obligates you, your heart must still be free. Let it be. Decisively cutting off people who are harming you is not cruel; it is safe and wise. Attend to it as far as you are able.

The pitfalls in distancing come along two lines: consideration of others and feeding the illusion. Physical distancing creates a vacuum. If you pull away from the manipulation, likely someone else will have to replace you. Your release may just guarantee someone else's bondage. Particularly if it is a parent-adult child relationship, your absence might only end up overburdening a sibling. Clearly, it is more responsible to share the load and find some strategy together. However it can be obtained, though, finding relief is vital.

The other pitfall of emotional distancing is more subtle. The strength you find in your haven may be enough to keep you alive, but also enough to convince onlookers that nothing is seriously wrong. If the manipulation is well isolated to private places, the illusion is already in place. The manipulator seems normal. And social situations may be the very havens from the pressure where you can breathe. If this is so, you will seem normal, too. Others notice nothing alarming and are lulled into false assumptions. If there is no display of your disgust or pain, people foolishly assume there is not any. They fail to realize that what they are seeing is not a sample of your manipulator's usual behavior, but a performance. Your very key to survival may be the very thing that is keeping you in bondage. Unknowingly, your haven, like appeasement, may be playing into the illusion of normalcy—so that when you need to turn to others for support, the public will be very reluctant to help.

Mr. and Mrs. Fanther have a thirteen-year-old daughter. Mr. Fanther has been making their lives difficult at home, but in public, he is amicable and amusing. Mother and daughter have found that going out with him is the one place they can be sure of getting some peace from the constant pressure and demands—he is happier when he is the center of attention. So they embrace the social events because they can relax and behave normally without fear. They are profoundly relieved to have those moments of peace and do not even consider what others may be thinking about it all.

Mind Games

Tackling manipulation head-on is not something most people are prepared to do. It is far easier to assume that the problem arises from some other more manageable source, even if that source is our own minds. We desperately want there to be some explanation that makes all this chaos understandable and all right. Hence, we can begin to play mind games with ourselves. They can come in a variety of forms, but here are a few:

• *Believing the illusion:* Everything is exactly the way it appears to be on the outside. The hidden behavior is normal and should not be upsetting you.

• *Contentment exercises:* These involve long arguments between your heart and mind in an effort to talk yourself into being happy. Things are not as bad as they could be. If you just overlook the nagging evil, you will be able to be happy with whatever residual good you might find.

• *Martyrdom:* This is a glorified victim mentality. It assumes that the suffering is accomplishing some purpose higher than what you understand. Rising up to fight it would turn you into the aggressor and the wicked one (at least by appearances).

• *Excuses:* This game makes the reason behind the gross behavior all-significant. Even though the violations may be serious, the explanations for them are understandable, so all consequences should be excused. Somehow the offender should be pitied, not censored, even if he has no regret at all.

• *Pretending:* This romanticizes the circumstances so that they appear reasonable or even heroic.

Vivian is married to a man who has grown increasingly demanding and irritable. Not only of her, but also of their children. She reasons, "Maybe he is dying of a wasting illness, but he doesn't want me to know. The manipulation that gets us to take on his responsibilities is just his way of secretly preparing us to survive without him."

- *Upside-down Thinking:* This is an effort to redefine right and wrong. It calls good bad and bad good. It says such things as, "This trial is good because it is somehow making me stronger, even if I do feel weaker" or "My comfort is bad for me because it leads to laziness."
- *Blind Faith:* This ignores patterns to trust in an empty hope that this time will be different.

Rewriting reality as something else does not change reality. The mind games, convincing yourself that something is different from what it really is, can be comforting. It can be a method of surviving psychologically overwhelming situations, but in the end, they are only mind games. You know it is not going to be good no matter how much you convince yourself that it might be good. If you actually begin to believe they are anything more than mind games, you are in grave danger of madness.

Psychological tricks are a favorite fallback answer to problems that seem to have no feasible solution. If we can change how we see a problem, then the problem may not be so daunting. This may be true for turmoil that originates in the mind, but there are other types of turmoil that do not. While it seems reasonable because it is open-minded, there really is no evidence of good coming from the hardship. External problems require external solutions. Thinking away starvation does not work. Food does.

No matter how ineffective, mind games do two things to help a victim of manipulation. One, they create distractions; and two, they prove that you are willing to consider the full range of possible solutions. By considering that the problem originates in your mind and not from somewhere else, you are showing an open-mindedness that might come in handy against future accusations. It proves that before creating an upheaval, you *did* look into your own heart first. The pitfall is, of course, that there is no real answer there. The facts will not align with the assumptions you will have to make. No matter how insistent you may become at trying to fit a square peg into a round hole, reality will tell. The answer is not there. And now you have given the problem even more time to grow even deeper roots.

Just Look Happy

While hardly a coping mechanism because it burdens more than it relieves, this is often an avenue that is considered. Theories that by changing your outward presentation or behavior, your inner well-being improves are rampant. Smile more. Sit up straight. Look people in the eye. Dress well. Walk with confidence. Compliment others. Breathe from the diaphragm. Exercise daily. Make eating healthy a priority. Be positive. While all of these are likely excellent advice in their place, they are not going to touch the real issue when dignity has been stripped. Something far more significant is necessary first, regardless of who claims otherwise. Instead of trying to talk yourself into self-respect, you will need to rise up to earn it.

By considering these theories, there is some distant wish that they will lend you strength. If you act confidently, it might counter the bold manipulation a little and get him to back down. After all, this thing should not have this much power over you. No one is supposed to be able to touch your self-respect and joy. It sounds reasonable. But if your confidence is not genuine, a manipulator can easily spot its superficiality. He will not be intimidated, and your energy will be sorely wasted. The sheer strain of acting so contrary to the strong negative emotions inside of you can be torturous. And in addition, it continues to mask the real problem to all those around.

But without looking happy, the victim mentality often aggravates oppression. Being used and keeping quiet about it eventually is not enough. Just bearing it is insufficient to his purpose. Your obvious suffering suggests that you are being severely wronged, even if you say nothing. This can enrage the manipulator. It is undermining his illusion, which may lead to more intense oppression. If he can, instead he will press you into acting like you like it, try to convince you that you are supposed to like it, or at least insist that you must endure it without showing any symptoms. Bear it, and *grin*. He must look good. Acting happy then just becomes a form of appeasing him.

Vivian believes she is struggling with self-confidence at work, so she has been reading up on how to boost it. She has been arriving early, dressing for success, and been proactive and positive, as much as she does not feel like it. For months, this act has been a strain and so far has not been paying off—she still gets overworked. One day, she is feeling too discouraged to pretend, and it shows, so her boss, Miss Abner, pulls her aside to reprimand her for her attitude because the CEO could make a surprise visit anytime.

So again, the options do not look promising. The pitfalls certainly outweigh the benefits, though they might sound reasonable at the time. You are fairly exploring avenues, and it does offer temporary protection. It may ease the worries of others, and it gives a different point of focus. But acting healthy when you are clearly not still does not solve anything and only spends energy you could be using more wisely elsewhere.

Perseverance

When all else fails: endure. Patient long-suffering is the default strategy of a victim mentality. If the above four options have been exhausted and found wanting, perseverance still stands. It may even seem to be the reasonable choice. After all, you may be personally tormented, but at least it is not bothering anyone else. It may seem noble—you are being loyal and faithfully carrying out your role, despite the suffering. It has the fragrance of virtue but, in this case, rarely the fruit.

You may notice that you keep getting crushed, but somehow you find the strength to recover. The less you think about the pain and injustice, the less agony there is. Plow through the agonizing duties as if they were justly yours and move on. One step at a time. Looking behind is too depressing; looking ahead is too overwhelming. Do now or die.

In the meantime, though, the pitfall is that you look like a devoted follower of the cause. People could even admire you for your loyalty, believing only firm conviction would drive you to such self-sacrifice. Instead of offering sympathy, they may even glorify your position— which, again, feeds the illusion.

Maurice lives on his family's homestead next to a small Civil War cemetery out in the country. For generations, his family has voluntarily kept up the grounds for the county. But Maurice is getting elderly, and yard maintenance is very taxing on his health. When requesting the county to take over the responsibility, he was told that it was not in the budget. Instead, they only praised him for upholding a noble tradition. His self-sacrifice is a tribute to the memory of the men buried there. He was even honored at the following Memorial Day ceremony. So Maurice keeps mowing.

The essential trouble with coping mechanisms is that they do not tackle the problem at its source. They just make it possible for you to stay victimized longer. The most seasoned diver can only hold his breath for so long, and then he must drown or fight to get air. For deeply ingrained wickedness (which alone may be a battle to label in your own mind), the only way to destroy it is to uproot it all. Messy, unpopular, disruptive, expensive, risky—yes!!! But necessary, alas. The best you can expect from coping is to temporarily avoid additional pain or shame, but the grueling sacrifice certainly does not bless anyone. It may effectively negate some harm, but it does not stop it from coming indefinitely. Putting out fires is noble and exhausting work, but it is more necessary to take down the pyromaniac. Leave the fires to burn for a while so that you can focus on the cause. Everyone will be better for it. You must endure what you cannot change, but you must also change what you can no longer endure.

By facing the obstacles in your own mind, you are more prepared to face the obstacles that will arise from others. The first step in the transformation from a victim to a survivor is to determinedly choose to fight for yourself. It is not selfish; it is responsible. You have value that needs to be upheld for the world to be a better place. You have experiences and skills that should be invested into worthwhile projects rather than spent irresponsibly on fruitless schemes someone else presses you into doing. Drop the shame that is not yours, face that which is and then leave it behind, and begin to battle for something better.

Manipulation's Counterattack

Taking a stand for yourself and for your protection is a threat to manipulation and control. Likely, even in the early stages of your awareness, a manipulator will recognize this and begin his counterattack. Many strategies of coercion, diversion, distortion, and division that you have not noticed before will arise. There will be a desperate effort to regain control, if not in one area then at least in another. Where there may not have been intimidation or harassment before, these new dimensions may arise. They will be disconcerting. You may not be prepared to handle this new intensity of pressure. You may even lose some ground for a while. There will be a tremendous temptation to give it up as not worth the fight. Yet if you are ever going to be able to overcome being a victim, these are going to have to be faced. Seeing clearly is your best safeguard. Understanding the manipulation, its motivations, and its strategies empowers you to effectively counter the lies that come from that source. Study the tactics, new and old. Develop a strategy. And stick to it firmly.

These attacks, which likely have marked your entire relationship, are really not new. The same lies still underlie the manipulative tactics. Just be prepared for the new affronts that arise when your focus changes from enduring to battling. The fight will likely become more overt, possibly involving additional people to support his stance. This additional battlefront may make the victim mentality all the more attractive. While certainly more intense, what you are fighting to protect is still far more valuable than his illusions. Once you know this, face them with boldness and confidence.

The Contribution of Others to the Victim Mentality

Oddly enough, other people play a large role in the victim mentality. In a position of weakness and self-doubt, we often rely heavily on the attitudes and opinions of others, especially those nearby. They are who we turn to to trust when we feel we cannot trust ourselves. They are a source of stability when we find ourselves off-balance. They are our link to a greater objectivity and a significant factor in how we view our situation. If those around you see you as someone who is being treated unfairly and in need of help, you are more likely to have the courage to rise up and fight. If, however, they see you as being in a position of your own making, a victim mentality can easily take root.

There are several levels of onlookers, most of them perfectly well-meaning. Some of them might even be heroic. But unless they too are acting with shrewdness and strategy, they too are vulnerable to being ignorantly drawn into the dance. Their efforts become futile also, and you all will be worse off for their help. So beware of these people; they will only drive you back into being a victim:

The Peacemakers

Carefully constructed illusions, for the very sake of misleading the general population, are not reality. What others see is a contrived version, so their opinions are not a good source of objectivity. After all, you have been making choices that appear to be your own. Apparently, they were of your own free will to achieve a purpose that you personally desired. The threats to the more precious core values that you are *actually* protecting are not noticeable. Manipulation sees that the illusions cover themselves well. As a result, your true motivations are buried under a heavy weight of confusion, shame, and fear. So already, you are largely misunderstood.

This careful disguise of reality makes making a fair judgment difficult for all parties. It leads many bystanders to take a neutral stance when they discover there is a conflict. It is the easy choice and perhaps wisest, at first. If they do get involved, though, peacemaking only plays into the manipulation. It assumes both parties are reasonable and interested in compromise. This in itself gives manipulation an unfair advantage, however unintentionally. He is not really interested in changing, but only in getting you to change. Whatever will add to the push toward this agenda is golden. He is seasoned at being unaffected by pressure himself, so there is no threat there. All that is generally required of him is just enough superficial agreement to appear willing. Rarely will there be any follow-up of his progress. If there happens to be, he can resort to any number of manipulative schemes to redirect attention back to you. He, unmoved, appears be compromising; while you, just gaining strength to stand firmly, appear stubborn. So the manipulator is often *very* enthusiastic about the shallow interest of others. It contributes to his goal—moving you. When even those who claim to be helping are harming, it is tempting to resign yourself to being the victim.

Frank has been acting depressed at work, and his coworker, Theresa, is concerned. With a little prodding, she finds that he is having marital troubles. So she gets Frank to invite her to dinner, where she meets his wife, Tessa. Tessa, just learning to unmask Frank's manipulation, must endure Theresa's tales of fights and reconciliations with her late husband, unsolicited advice about relationships, and sugary offers to become her confidential friend. Frank is all ears and acts very grateful for her wisdom. Tessa, though she cannot yet put it into words, is repulsed by the entire situation and must emphatically put her foot down after Theresa repeatedly ignores her polite refusals. Theresa and Frank exchange meaningful looks of helpless frustration on her way out.

The Concerned

Other bystanders may be reluctant to offend the manipulator. These are the people who are willing to look at the situation more fairly but are hesitant to take a stand. Offending a staunch manipulator is a dangerous business. They can easily fall victim to his schemes also, especially if they have a history with him. Since he is free from the confines of integrity, their energy, position, reputation, freedom, and identity are not at all sacred, either. They know this and have no intention of risking their well-being. Far better to handle him with kid gloves and justify it as giving him the benefit of the doubt. For the sake of self-preservation, it is easier to dismiss the victim than to disturb a sleeping beast.

While completely understandable, this also contributes to the victim's helplessness. Their silence suggests that they see nothing significantly wrong. If the daunting threats are enough to keep them from just speaking up, when they have far less at stake, then they are daunting enough to keep another soul imprisoned. If those with insight, strength, and resources feel ill-equipped to fight, how much more the one who has been stripped of all those things?

Mrs. Gunley lives next door to a man and his seventeen-year-

old son, Jay. She has listened to the angry yelling through the walls of the apartment for years, but only in the father's voice. She notices Jay walks as if he is carrying a heavy burden but tries his best to be pleasant to her in the hall. Mrs. Gunley is concerned, but she is elderly, and no one really listens to her anyway. Jay's father is very intimidating, so she says nothing. She reasons Jay will be eighteen in another year, so he can get out soon enough on his own.

The people that notice a problem are the victim's primary hope. If there is a refusal to help, it is abandonment. If those outside of the trap are too terrified to fight for fear of being caught themselves, there is little hope of a rescue. The victim mentality seems highly attractive then.

The Merciful

A third group of people are those who sense that something is not right and want to help but fail to know what to do. Usually, they notice that the situation is negative, though they may not understand the cause. This stirs them to pity, a pity that will shower you with gifts or attention or even service, but really does no tangible good. First, the shame of being pitied is a fairly heavy burden to bear alone. Having to depend on charity for survival is embarrassing, however grateful you may be for it. If accompanied by the need to repay the favor, the help is almost not worth accepting. More obligations are not at all welcome to someone who is already stretched too thin.

Secondly, the help may actually be enabling the manipulation. If you are at the end of your resources and someone comes to your aide, you make it through that time. It *is* a mercy. But if a manipulator is continuing to press you to your breaking point, you will need help again and again. Your new resources will be cheerfully exhausted, and you will be just where you were before. And the next time, though you can be sure the expectations have been raised, the help may not be there. So isolated help is not very helpful. You may even be left worse off than without the pity and left alone to suffer alone.

> *Gerald is married to Louise, an alcoholic. Though he works hard, she manages to spend most of their meager income on her addiction. When the car breaks down, a church member anonymously pays for the repairs. Gerald is immeasurably grateful, because now he will not lose his job. But Louise's family sees none of this and assumes that the couple is getting by just fine. After all, it is Gerald's responsibility to keep them afloat, and apparently, he is, so they do not need to say anything. But when the car breaks down again, Gerald is just as helpless as he was before. This time, there may not be an anonymous gift, though.*

Living on the edge is full of uncertainty. There is no real margin for error. Though you may have the strength to survive a fall over the edge (with or without the help of another), there is no telling when you will not. Accepting the mercy of others can be a blessing, but you know very well that it cannot be a lifestyle. Well-intended mercy, if not rightly given, can only extenuate your misery. This is bitter indeed.

The Empathizers

A fourth group of observers are those who have felt your pain a bit, likely with the same manipulator, and who can empathize. They are the big-hearted, self-sacrificing souls who are willing to subject themselves to the manipulation just to give you some relief from it. Often the situation is not entirely clear to them, but there is a sense that their presence helps to relieve a burden bigger than it would appear. Altruistically, they may even allow themselves to be taken advantage of to provide you some relief. This is pure nobility, but it does little ultimate good. In fact, if the usual victim sees that the manipulation is spreading to others, there may be a counter-self-sacrifice. You may be willing to suffer more burdens just to prevent other parties from being dragged into the manipulation also. It becomes a cycle of trying to relieve each other, while the manipulator sits back and benefits from you both! But if you do not realize this, being the victim is a heroic deed because now it is sparing others from your fate, too.

Andrea is a mother returning to work as a paralegal, anxious to prove herself in her new position under a highly successful attorney. She takes the responsibilities given to her seriously and does them to the best of her ability. The attorney recognizes this and loads her down with more and more significant duties. Andrea feels like their clients deserve her best efforts, but she still has responsibilities at home. Jessica, the seasoned receptionist, notices Andrea's struggle and intercepts some of the obligations that would naturally fall on Andrea. She knows Andrea would object, so she does not tell her. The attorney is delighted at this show of enthusiasm and gladly obliges with more work. Now they are both overloaded. And if Andrea catches on to what Jessica is doing, she will feel guilty for being incompetent and want to redouble her efforts to relieve the burden that Jessica is carrying for her.

While these reactions of bystanders are understandable, they are not really helpful. Knowing the dynamics is crucial to avoid feeding a damaging cycle. Anyone or anything that is lending power to the manipulation, however unintentionally, is a danger to you. If you are already weakened by the situation, trying to bear the additional burdens that others create is not at all helpful. They should be disregarded. You must learn to rely on your own judgment and on the help of those who are interested in genuinely supporting you personally. Politely ignore the rest.

The Voices of Minimization

Despite the counter-productive involvement of others, you may find the strength to speak out and ask for help. Absolutely this is crucial, but there too you will be met with unexpected opposition. You will be blamed for and shamed by the problem all over again. The lies and accusations will flood in again, only with different voices. If you have not heard them all from your manipulator or from your own thoughts already, you will likely hear them boldly voiced by others. As true as they may sound, beware, because they are still just lies.

Intense shame, especially when it is undeserved, is not an imaginary problem. Generally, this is obvious, regardless of how others may misunderstand or refuse to see it. There are physical, emotional, and social clues that there is some intense suffering occurring, far more than the superficial evidence might suggest. People recognize this, but how they respond to it, ironically, makes all the difference. If they respond appropriately, it is risky but life-giving. If they are looking to ignore the evidence, there are plenty of ways to dump the problem back onto you.

This mentality—though possibly disguised as nobility, higher understanding, helpful advice, or even superficial empathy—can greatly damage a suffering soul. Dismissal, in one form or another, minimizes the pain and suffering of he who is already enduring staggering shame. As well-meant as it may sound, it does no good. In fact, their words are likely doing far more damage than outright hostility would. Even if you understand that their efforts are directed more at soothing their own conscience than at solving a problem, the dismissal of the real suffering still leaves a wake of destruction. You are left with more shame and blame, more staggering burdens and rejection, more helplessness and hopelessness, and no real help. Maybe some of these voices sound familiar:

You are Crazy

"Clearly you have issues."

"Be reasonable. Don't blow this out of proportion."

"You are being hyper-sensitive."

"You're blinded by your hurt and anger."

"You're probably just hormonal."

"That does sound frustrating."

The assumption behind these comments is that you have failed to take everything into consideration. Somehow your vision is skewed, so your judgment is inferior. Because they can find some psychological explanation for your pain, your pleas can be easily dismissed. The issue is then just a problem with your mind, which does not require their sympathy, time, or investment. They may remain interested, perhaps approaching you as a scientific problem, but not involved. (How this world is plagued with far too many amateur psychologists and self-appointed counselors!) They are then free from any responsibility by claiming you are crazy. No sound individual will defend madness. And if you become convinced by them that your judgment is indeed misguided, then you can easily get trapped in a downward spiral of self-doubt, opening yourself to being even more thoroughly misused.

Counteraccusation

"You must understand that you are guilty, too."

"It was your choice to begin with, wasn't it?"

"You should have known what would happen."

"What did you do to provoke him?"

"Be careful where you point your finger because there are three others pointing back at you!"

"We all need to be put in our place from time to time."

"You hypocrite!"

Counteraccusations harshly present the opposite extreme. When faced with your claims, it turns the blame around so that you appear to be equally, if not more, guilty. This uses shame to justify shame. There are times when counteraccusations are absolutely appropriate. If there is an unreasonable insistence of complete innocence, then a good dose of harsh reality is appropriate. But with intense shame, dignity has been violated so far that any more shame is crushing—especially from the one you asked for help. Counteraccusations are aggressive and cruel if they are used on someone who is already helplessly broken.

Change Yourself

"You're not seeing it from his perspective."

"You don't understand what he's trying to do. It's visionary."

"Your standards are too high. Be fair."

"Count your blessings. It could always be worse."

"Roll with the punches. Learn to laugh it off. Forgive and forget."

"It might be hard right now, but you need to look at the possibilities."

"Try a little harder/a different approach."

"It sounds like it's just one of those normal challenges of life. We all face them. Buck up!"

"It's just a relationship challenge/gender difference/generation gap/ personality clash."

"Be a little more open-minded and you will see."

These are gentler prods than the counteraccusations, but they often carry just as much of a burden with them. The philosophy is that all relational issues can be solved by looking at them differently. Under normal circumstances, changing yourself can have profound effects. However, changing your attitude when there is an outside source of the problem rarely solves anything at all. Claiming that it should puts unfair burdens back on he who is suffering intensely already. It only diverts the individual to a side-eddy, which may even compound the trouble and certainly does not offer any real solution.

A challenge to change yourself is a dismissal by misdiagnosis: not of the mind, as "you are crazy," but of the spirit, "you are inflexible."

Diplomacy

"I'm not going to take sides."

"I'm just trying to be fair."

"Both of you will have to work this out."

"There are two sides to every story."

"You need to be the one to initiate the reconciliation. The sooner, the better."

The individual who makes these types of comments is determined to take the middle road. It is a dismissal by neutrality. There might be efforts to help, but the help will only come along the lines of finding a compromise. The assumption is that the truth lies somewhere in the middle, and both sides are going to have to give in a bit to meet there. Often, this is a *very* appropriate method of dealing with relational issues—just not always. Beware of those who tempt you to make peace at too great a cost. Advocating compromise presses the victim into more futile sacrifice that will still not achieve peace (unless annihilation of one of the parties is considered peace). Insisting on pulling down boundaries is exactly the wrong advice in the midst of an attack on a soul. They promote civility while refusing to recognize the seriousness of the injustice. When there are real violations of justice and freedom and dignity, the time for diplomacy has ended and a time for action has come. In war, a man of passion must take a side—diplomacy becomes not only an act of cowardice but also a dangerous philosophy.

Disbelief

"It can't be that bad."

"It doesn't look that bad to me."

"He's not dangerous."

"You seem okay."

Disbelief is probably the natural starting point for all hidden problems. People want what seems to be to be what is. And often times, it is. But disbelief is only a start. When there arises a doubt, it is necessary to search harder for truth. If disbelief stops at disbelief, it is nothing but a dismissal. If you have made an appeal to someone, you want them to weigh it as objectively as possible—with whatever research that might involve. But many won't. Disbelief can never be transformed back into comfortable ignorance, but that does not mean some people will not try. The most dangerous enemies are those who appear to be innocent. And the most harmful bystanders are those who refuse to acknowledge the danger.

Excusing It Away

"His behavior is understandable."
"Maybe he doesn't realize what he is doing."
"Everybody makes mistakes."
"He's hurting. Pity him and tolerate it."
"You probably didn't make yourself clear enough."

Excuses suggest that you have no reason for being miserable. Since they can find some reasonable explanation for his actions, there should not be any harmful consequences. It denies that his behavior has caused you harm and may even suggest that by experiencing the hurt, you are creating a problem yourself. Perhaps there is some truth in these claims to make them believable, but ignorance does not excuse guilt. Justice must follow from an offense. Just because there is an explanation means very little to the effects. If you have crashed your car into a tree, your car remains smashed. No matter why you happened to crash, damage has been done.

Theory Application

"You are hurt/shamed only as far as you allow yourself to be."
"You get out of a relationship only as much as you put into it."

"Happiness is a choice we make, completely independent of circumstances."

"It's nothing a little sacrificial love will not cure. Invest more."

"Don't let it bother you. Letting it bother you gives the other person power over you. It's your fault really for allowing yourself to feel that way."

"People who are abused are so only because they let themselves be. It's your problem. If you really wanted it to stop, you would stop it."

It seems a great deal of the population have some pet theory that they are anxious to test, at your expense. Theories sound good. They may even be sound. But they do nothing to answer a heart-cry. It assumes the problem can be addressed strictly by principle. It oversimplifies the situation and places a moral burden on someone who has no strength to weigh its validity, let alone bear it. Those who apply theory alone to solve someone else's staggeringly difficult problems ignore the emotional dimension. They use intellectual prowess to disguise accusations and pressures to change. It is a dismissal disguised as a solution. Perhaps at some point, these principles may be helpful or strengthening, but not until the individual is prepared—after the pain, shame, and confusion have been recognized and thoroughly sorted. Intense shame needs sympathy, not theory—a sympathy that does not feed self-pity but acknowledges the reality of the injustice and the legitimacy of the pain.

Menacing Challenge

"What's your evidence?"

"Are you certain you understand what the consequences of your accusations would be?"

"Have you realized who else you will be bothering by these claims?"

"You will regret whatever you're thinking of doing about it."

Menacing challenges aggressively attack an emotional issue with legal strategies. They reduce the problem to one of cold facts and figures, where emotions have little solid defense. Shame cannot be scientifically measured. It is not possible to calculate how much trouble restoring dignity is worth in financial terms or man-hours or inconvenience to others. How much is a life worth? While the life that is being saved may not be from physical death, it is a rescue from a lifeless life. People *are* worth saving; and it is a true hero who recognizes this. These types of confrontational challenges, while possibly points to consider, are only a sliver of the entire issue. A rescue always involves a risk; but should the intimidation of these risks prevent a rescue?

Complete Dismissal
"This too shall pass. Time will heal all wounds."
"Be careful! Don't be a gossip."
"Leave the dead past behind. What's done is done."
"Well, every cloud has a silver lining."
"If it will help you feel better, you can tell me about it."
"I don't know what to tell you to do."
"I don't know anything about it."
"Listen to my tale, too..."
"I don't want to get involved."

Ironically, complete dismissals are the most humane of all the minimization tactics. There is really no pretense of help, little effort to add additional burdens, and no significant shifting of responsibility. The complete lack of concern may be stabbing, but at least there is no confusion where the individual stands. Rather than being led along down false paths of freedom and aide, no direction is offered at all. The population at large is wise to keep out of a disagreement, especially when they are ignorant of the details. If they are unwilling to research further, they ought to stay out of it altogether. So indeed, this is far more merciful than any of the others.

In all probability, you have already encountered these arguments. A skilled manipulator will have been using them, at least by implication, for years. A conscientious person will have exhausted these possibilities before pleading for help. Finding an answer within yourself is much less disruptive than appealing to others, especially for indistinct problems. Self-blame *is* the easier option. So often you have already been swimming around in the subjective soup for a very long time, completely unable to find a satisfactory solution. These arguments simply do not satisfy the facts. And now, when you have finally found the courage to consider an objective explanation of right and wrong, you are only shoved back down with indifferent advice from those who likely have never lost their dignity.

The minimization of intense shame is like a death sentence. In essence, it says to a mortally wounded soldier reaching out with the last of his strength, "Shut up and sit down." Though the words presented may be entirely legitimate under different circumstances, they are worse than a flood of hate to the victimized. Their partial truths stab a broken will who is just groping for someone to acknowledge that their existence is not normal and that there is something *fundamentally* wrong. Behind the words, the message "I will not support or love you through this" is utterly staggering. It completely dismisses the spirit of the plea and devalues your freedom and dignity. It is abandonment in a garb of sound counsel; you are considered not worth a fight. And why? Likely simply because it is safer for them to dismiss you than offend him. It is the path of least resistance.

If you are being fed this garbage, do not swallow it! You may even be feeding it to yourself. But your judgments are not so skewed that you cannot taste the difference between bitterness and sweetness. You have been mistreated. It *is* a real problem. If you are struggling just to achieve some minimal level of dignity and voices keep pushing you back, there *is* something fundamentally wrong. And it is not you.

The expressions of the minimization of shame can be paralyzing, but you must believe that there is a significant number of people who understand, who are willing to support you, who have been where you are, and who know that this is no trivial matter. It *is* a cause to fight, and they will fight beside you. Just because they have not found you yet is no evidence that they do not exist. Reach out, however feebly, because we *are* here!

Between the increased pressures, voices of shame, coping pitfalls, and the contributions of others, however well-intended, being victimized might appear to be the only option. All superficial help is mostly useless, if not counterproductive. Real help is risky and requires tremendous personal investment. If you do not already have people who are willing to support you through this, establishing those relationships may be overwhelming in itself. It is going to take a great deal of time to build trust, and then it is still uncertain if they will be willing to stand by you in the end. Even finding a professional who understands can be a daunting search. But do it anyway. You are worth it.

6
REDISCOVERING DIGNITY DESPITE THE ODDS

EVERY HUMAN BEING HAS WORTH. You are valuable for who you are. Those things that make you unique—your personality, your skills, your experiences—however imperfect, can be used to make a positive impact on this broken world. Your thoughts, emotions, desires, dreams, and perspective are all important factors in what makes you you. They are not so valueless that they should be overwritten for anyone else's purpose. Though at times they must be put aside for a greater good, they are not meant to be abandoned indefinitely. If you are asked to, politely decline. There is no one who should be mastered by another.

Dignity is a gift to humanity. It is the basic respect due every human being. It acknowledges that you have value, that your contributions matter. It says that you have great potential worthy of investment—investment of time, resources, and others. It reminds you of your significance and helps you to discover your purpose. It draws out the goodness inside of you that enriches your life and those of others around you. And once it is embraced, it fuels greatness. But in order to be healthy, dignity needs to be fed a little respect. It must have the freedom to be what it is.

But when freedom is threatened, so is dignity. They both must be protected. To properly protect them requires tremendous strength, insight, and vigilance, especially in the face of constant bombardment. When the stabs of manipulation pierce deeply enough for long enough, the strength wanes. If the defenses are already weakened by shame, despair creeps in. When the will gets too broken to protect its dignity, then all sorts of troubles invade. All that was once noble is threatened, and what should not be taken or surrendered may very well be.

What you need if you have become a victim of manipulation is strength. Strength that comes from clarity of mind, determination of will, dedication of heart, and support. These are things that you cannot generate or imagine yourself into. You must take steps to develop them and get stronger. It is a process. You will have to stretch yourself beyond what you think you can do. With failure comes insight; with success comes confidence—confidence in your abilities, in the effectiveness of the principles, in truth. Confidence is the great dispeller of doubt, which is your biggest liability in the manipulation game. Apply wisdom and confidence to shed the subtle lies.

Shame

The opposite of dignity is shame. Shame, in its healthy form, is actually designed to protect dignity. It is like pain. If your fingers get slammed in a door, your nerves send warning signals to your brain that there is a problem and the situation needs to change. So you listen and pull them out. Similarly, when there a social violation, shame is often sent our way in order to get us to correct it. Say a piece of spinach is stuck in your teeth. There is shame, and there is a signal to your brain to fix it. Unfortunately, the signal is often in the form of another person, which is embarrassing, but it is still a signal. Something ought to be done to change the situation. And often you do. So the social *faux pas* is remedied.

When shame is not handled properly, however, it can build up and wreak havoc. It might be ignored, covered, or shamelessly flaunted, but somehow it is not faced for what it is. The warning is not heeded, and no steps are taken to take care of the real issue. So problems begin to compound.

Both the manipulator and his victim are struggling to process shame properly, only the nature of their errors is *vastly* different. The manipulator is interested in keeping control. Shame then reflects a vulnerability, which endangers that control. If he is seen as weak, then he cannot command the situation as well. Instead, he scrambles to deny that there is any reason for the shame. And unfortunately, when manipulation is no obstacle, the consequences are not limited to himself.

Covering it up is an automatic response to shame and is sometimes a healthy way of dealing with it. We wear clothes and deodorant to cover our shame, a shame that we cannot manage any other way. But covering shame that ought to be brought into the open is damaging. Drug problems, financial struggles, and mental issues are examples of shameful conditions that need help, not hiding. Continuing to cover such things up only invites them to grow worse and worse. But if covering it up becomes too much, manipulation has several other options.

Denial is a common first effort to disregard shame. Simply refusing to acknowledge that it is there appears to let them off easily. It suggests that if you are disturbed by the situation, then that is your own problem. Your judgment, not the circumstances, is what is off. Then you might scramble to try to deal with the problem as best as you can, but you are unable to make any real progress toward fixing it without his cooperation. It is then tempting to pretend along with him that nothing is wrong.

Your boss comes in last minute for your group presentation to the board. He is the key speaker of your group in a small conference room and has clearly eaten raw onions for lunch. You discretely mention to him that he might want a mint. He states aloud, "That is not necessary," while you try to suppress a cringe from the odor.

Blaming clearly draws someone else into the issue. Somehow, it becomes someone else's fault that there is a problem, so it is not his to fix. If you are the one being blamed, it is now your problem. In good faith, you ought to try to correct your contribution to the problem. But when the blame keeps coming, it can be difficult to know what to do. This confusion might drive you to scramble. But no matter how you adjust your behavior, the blame does not stop because the source of the shame is not addressed. And it isn't because of you.

You quietly duck out to get some breath fresheners from your desk. You try to offer him one under the table, but he refuses. "You're the one that scheduled this for right after lunch," he blames in a low tone. You make a mental note to schedule meetings in the mornings from now on.

Altering perception is another tactic, which now becomes clearly manipulative. By publicly overshadowing his shame with yours, he can shift the focus. Now you are helplessly left to handle it or be judged for not trying to. Turning the accusation back upon the guilty party is often just as shameful, so you are trapped.

While you pocket the breath fresheners and get up to turn the scent diffuser up to high, your boss jokes to everyone, "It looks like someone has an odor issue." All eyes turn to you. Sheer mortification silences you, but you do manage a weak smile. You back to the wall at the far side of the room and begin to count the minutes.

Hiding is also an unhealthy method for dealing with shame. If the other methods appear to be failing, then it is often a simple matter to just disappear. If those who remind him of his shame are not around, there is no feeling of shame. He can go on as if nothing is wrong. Manipulators are known to switch loyalties easily once their behavior starts to be widely known in a given crowd.

By your staying at the opposite side of the room, the members of the board begin to suspect the source of the strong onion scent. Once meaningful nose twitches are exchanged between them, your boss abruptly says, "And I'll let my assistant take it from here. 'Always give the underdog a chance' is my motto." And the door slams on his way out.

The manipulator's mistake is in rejecting real shame. Rather than accepting it and facing the problem that it signifies, he shifts things around to make it disappear. He makes it appear that it is not his lack of character that has led to a mess, but some other factor outside of his control. So his shame is diverted. But in reality, it is still very much there. He has only distanced himself from it, often leaving someone else to clean up the mess. But it is still his. This subtle difference is easy to miss, though, which leads to the victim's troubles with processing shame...

As the healthier person, you probably know that shame ought to be faced and fixed. And, with all of the garbage flying at you, you have tried. But the shame and blame do not stop. The more you try to face the shame that falls upon you, it really never goes away. So reasonable people of goodwill resort to other methods for dealing with it. There might be efforts to work off the shame by being especially good or perfect, trying to counteract the disgrace with worthy deeds. You might just try to endure it, accepting shame as a part of life and hoping it doesn't cause too much disruption. Shame might also be transferred into guilt—somehow your failure is so wrong that you deserve to feel completely miserable about it for the rest of your life. Gnawing regret is your just consequence. Or suppression, which means trying to talk your heart into believing that it does not matter.

The truth is that shame can only be properly handled by he who has created it. Shame from lack of resources, influence, understanding, or strength is not legitimate shame. Shame from lack of character is. So the manipulator is rapidly generating shame, which he recognizes only long enough to unload onto you and others. And then you are left holding a mess that is impossible for you to fix properly. You cannot improve someone else's character. While you cannot force the manipulator to deal with his own shame and error, you no longer need to accept it when it is unjustly dumped onto you.

Despite how outsiders might view the situation, it is not yours. Know it for yourself. Deal with what small pieces might be your contribution and *leave the rest alone!* (The truth will eventually sort itself out.)

You cannot begin to reclaim your dignity until the influx of undeserved shame stops. False shame *ought* to be denied, rejected, and left alone. Your rejection of it is not shamelessness but a determination to be unashamed. Seeing it for what it is is absolutely vital. It may never stop pouring out, but at least you can keep it from pouring into you.

Human Needs

As humans, we have needs—legitimate needs. Getting those

needs met is an important part of maintaining dignity. Often in times of stress, pressures squeeze out the opportunities to meet those needs. This is part of life. But when the pressure is prolonged, the unmet needs become gaping holes. This erodes self-worth and is often the beginning of a downward spiral to despair, poverty, disease, or other social ills. Though rising up to meet the need is important to healing, awareness and prevention is better.

With manipulations' inclination to blur lines, they often push others farther than is healthy. Asking a little at a time may find you giving far too much without understanding how you got there. There is an ache and an emptiness that was not so deep before. This is an unmet need. It is wise to take note of the symptoms. Your mind and body usually tell you when there is something wrong. In general, physical needs have physical warnings, emotional needs have emotional warnings, and psychological needs have psychological warnings. Negative feelings are signs that something is empty. It is advisable to take heed.

The best thing to do with an ache is to step back with objectivity. You are human, with human needs. Figure out what is missing. Failing to meet those needs for brief periods of time can be noble or character building. It may be strengthening. What we do not gain in comfort, we often gain in character. However, failing to meet those same needs over extended periods of time will end in a handicap. It weakens. It might be heroic to endure the pain of a deep wound during the trip to the hospital, but once you reach help, it is equally important to accept it. Your life may depend on it. The real need does need to be addressed.

Knowing your needs and the signs of deprivation is important. Evaluating yourself from a more objective viewpoint reveals that you *should* receive some benefit from life. It is not about being selfish or expecting special benefit, but it is about meeting a minimum standard for well-being. Seasons of life and circumstances may press us to do with less than is ideal for a time, but the goal should be to restore them to healthy levels. If something or someone is in the way, it is important to make plans to move the obstacle.

Satisfying a need requires something from the outside to come in to help you have life, health, or dignity. Often this means that you will have to reach outside of yourself to get the need met. But there is usually something you must invest as well. The bathtub will not come to you. When you are dirty, you must invest some effort into getting clean yourself, though soap and water are essential ingredients also. If the resources or cooperation are absent in one way, search elsewhere. Likely there are other avenues for meeting the need.

The following chart illustrates some of these needs, what the warning signs might look like to signal the need is not being met, one way the need might be met, and what happens if it continues to be left unmet. The physical ones, being straightforward, are easy to understand. They make good parallels to their often-misunderstood counterparts. Other types of want need to be addressed, too.

Need	Low Fuel Signal	To Fulfill Need	Result if Left Unmet
Physical			
Food	Hunger	Eat	Starvation
Drink	Thirst	Drink	Dehydration
Sleep	Fatigue	Sleep	Collapse
Clothing	Cold, immodesty, scrubbiness	Obtain clothing	Nakedness
Shelter & adequate atmospheric conditions	Sweat, shivers, sluggishness	Obtain shelter	Shutdown of bodily functions
Health/medical attention	Pain, blood, discoloration, etc.	Proper treatment	Illness/Maiming
Hygiene	Dirt, smell	Bathe, etc.	Disease
Rest	Weariness	Rest	Exhaustion
Physical stimulation	Lethargy	Exercise	Lack of strength
Physical safety	Fear, alerts	Get to a safe place	Harm
Physical non-dependence	Disability	Get a physical therapy coach	Inability
Emotional			
Socialization	Loneliness	Visit people	Exile
Affection	Overly savor crumbs	Touch (respectfully)	Compromised chastity
Respect	Solo service	Stand for truth	Futility
Mercy	Walking on eggshells	Insist on margin	Hopelessness
Peace/Relaxation	Screaming (internal or external)	Find a haven	Insanity
Affirmation/Acceptance	Stoniness	Find a friend	Artificiality
Happiness/Pleasure	Melancholy	Do something enjoyable	Despair
Emotional safety	Stress	Get to a safe place	Chronic anxiety
Emotional non-dependence	Insecurity	Get a support group	Hysteria

Need	Low Fuel Signal	To Fulfill Need	Result if Left Unmet
Psychological			
Work/Purpose	Idleness	Get a job	Uselessness
Satisfaction in work/Success	Discouragement	Change jobs	Sloppiness
Resources to accomplish responsibilities	Shortcuts	Ask for help	Shame
Rest from work	Haggardness	Vacation	Slavery
Justice	Anger	Appeal to an authority	Revenge
Mental stimulation	Boredom	Develop interests	Empty conversation
Boundaries/ Mental safety	Helplessness	Allow consequences	Being abused
Psychological non-dependence	Indecision	Get a confidence coach	Being manipulated
Spiritual *			
Forgiveness	Guilt	Grace	Eternal punishment
Communion with God	Indifference	Pray	Alienation
Corporate worship	Absence	Go to church	Disconnection
Theological grounding	Confusion	Learn from others	Distortion
Sound philosophy	Directionlessness	Find answers	Error
Spiritual safety	Isolation	Fellowship	Dullness
Spiritual non-dependence	Mimicry	Find evidence of power	Mediocrity

*Adjust these according to your faith.

Manipulation often infers with this process. Strength comes from having your needs met. If you can be diverted into fueling his agenda instead, this is clearly to his benefit. You are weakened while he is strengthened. And it is tyranny. It compels you to give to him from your needs to fill his own—you meet his needs at your expense, and it costs you dearly. Though your symptoms may be obvious, they will likely be disregarded. Enemies do not want you strong but weak. So it is important to know what your needs are objectively so that you can stand up to defend them yourself. Life is worth protecting; invest a little into your own.

Strong Enough to Stand

Holding onto dignity is often a struggle, no matter how much it should not be one. There are forces—some cultural, some social or political, some practical—that often even unknowingly usurp life and liberty from someone somehow. Resisting the harmful effects is not always easy. Discerning when, how, and to what extent opposition is needed can be difficult to judge. But when something higher than mere comfort is a stake, there needs to be resistance—if not initially in word and action, certainly in will. Heed the natural repulsion to that which is not right. Despite the opposition, be determined to side with what is just and true beyond the muddling. And this means standing strong with conviction.

There are different types of strength. There is strength of character, personality, mind, might, influence, power, word, and endurance. As long as you are breathing, you are demonstrating some strength; you are at least struggling against the elements to physically survive. Under different circumstances, the elements working against our health and well-being come in different forms and require different battle strategies and different types of strength. In actual war, might is most necessary. In debate, the mind. In persuasion, the personality. In suffering, endurance. But the type of strength that you are currently demonstrating neither defines who you are nor what you must continue to do. If what you are trying to do is not working, perhaps a different approach is necessary. And a new strategy may require a shift in strength. Exercise the weaker muscles. And with a little creativity, it is possible to apply even your skilled strengths in a different combination to engage the current battle well.

There is tremendous power in focused effort—even yours. Once you have become convinced that there is a powerful and destructive force warring against you, you need to begin to unearth it. Nothing tremendous at first, just a simple independence of thought. Refusing to be so easily moved is a good start. And you will find that, though in a good relationship this is just a standard application of give-and-take; to control, this is intolerable.

Especially with manipulation, more distortion and diversions are certain to come. They may come from well-meaning or ill-meaning sources, but they are always disguised as good. Likely they will seem right at the time. Know that not all paths are created equal. There are some that have dangerous pitfalls; others will cost those you love more than they should. Consequently, not all opinions of the best path are created equal, either. Know that just because you are judged, it does not mean the judgment is just. Stand on what you have determined is right objectively, when there was no pressure to decide. Defaulting to a neutral or safer position is often wise in uncertainty. Buy some time to think more clearly. It is important to keep standing, regardless of how you may be accused.

You Have a Purpose

You have dignity, you have needs, you have strength, and you have purpose. Purpose moves us forward toward a particular goal. It gives meaning, hope, and direction to the journey of life. Though circumstances may redirect you, and your purpose may be adjusted, there is still a goal to reach toward. It helps to both express and shape your identity. And it should be one that you personally believe in. Where you spend your most time, energy, and support must be something you consider worthwhile—regardless of what your manipulator thinks. No obligation is so important that your purpose should be rewritten to meet it. Your investment is valuable and should be carefully committed to trustworthy causes only.

Manipulation cannot technically harm your potential, but it can destroy your effectiveness. You cannot achieve your purpose until you can focus your best efforts in that direction, with dedication and zeal. If your strength is being usurped for lesser things, particularly those you do not even believe are leading to ultimate good, your purpose is being derailed. You are ineffective. Shed the tangled obligations that lead to no significant good. What you have to offer without it is far better than anything you can accomplish against your better judgment or will. Live in abundance, with joy, toward what you really care about. Your life needs to count for something. Fight to get to that point, where you can begin living up to all you can become.

While you may not know your purpose or it may seem too impossible to achieve any longer, you likely have some inkling. It usually lies along the lines of your dreams, talents, and interests. And it incorporates your experiences—good and terrible. There is a niche you can fill, and your investments can matter. Finding it is a journey always, but one that can wait a bit. For now, it is less important that you have defined it than that you know it exists. Resigning yourself to control just because your purpose is still left undefined is unwise. Mediocrity is no purpose. Just because you do not have vision at the moment does not imply that you do not have potential. Fight for freedom so that you can find your purpose.

Even if you do not do it for yourself, do the right thing by those who are depending on you, who have genuinely sacrificed for you, who have fought for you, who believe in you, who love you. Those who love you best see what is best for you, even if you do not value it so much. People who genuinely love you will not let you destroy yourself in foolish sacrifice for empty principles that do not produce fruit. Hope, however indistinct, is brighter than despair. Trust a little in the vision they have for your restoration. They believe in you for good reason.

Value of Freedom

Your dignity needs to be respected, protected, and secured. Democratic societies understand this and generally try to uphold the lives and dignity of their citizens. They fight to establish and protect freedom: freedom of thought, freedom of speech, freedom of religion, freedom of choice, freedom of movement, freedom from want, freedom from fear. Freedoms secure dignity, which often means a fight. So fight we must, because human dignity is *that* important.

But when the system fails, when injustice is hidden in the shadows and indignity is rampant, when you suffer alone and there is no one to defend you—you still deserve dignity. Even if you are the only one who knows there is oppression, do what you need to do to regain it. Fight for the freedoms you need to secure it. As far as you can, break free from the bonds of oppression: mentally, emotionally, spiritually, financially, and physically. You can only know peace to the extent of your freedom. Where it is not given, it must be won.

Breaking free is going to require ingenuity, initiative, and strength. If you are coming from a victim mentality, these things can seem impossible. But they are indeed within you. Sort through the obligations, expectations, roles, fears, and other triggers that have gotten you stuck. Discard the ones that have proven unbeneficial. Make room for those that add richness to your life. Test your suspicions and draw fair conclusions from the results. As much as there should not be a threat to your freedom, there is one—so you will have to fight for it. Make it a good one.

Just remember, one individual's freedom cannot be won at the expense of another's. You cannot violate someone else's dignity—even your oppressor's—in striving for your own. As tempting as it may be to offer him a taste of his own medicine, but it does not offer basic respect. Goodness fights without meanness or deceit. To secure *everyone's* natural rights, the resistance must be made with steady insistence, respect, and demonstration of character. Do not become like him in your battle against him. In its bold response to injustice, standing strong draws out truth. Unfortunately, it is often an ugly truth that people may not want to face, which can drive them to become unpleasant. The shame of it all needs to speak for itself; it needs no amplification from you. Step back and let it be exposed. Ugly injustice is threatened most by calm truth because the contrast is so stark. Strive for this end.

This can be a difficult balance to maintain, especially when you are pressed to take action. But firstly, it is more important to escape the prison that he has built in your mind. Allow yourself to dream a little. You do not have to settle for being mastered. The grass *is* greener on the other side. The overwhelming odds are worth fighting against. The hope is rich enough to risk what little you do have to try and reach it. Freedom is key to your dignity, your life, your purpose. Trust a little in the vision, even if it is still fuzzy, because it *is* possible to taste joy again.

7
EMBRACING REALITY

Bold confidence must be met with equally bold confidence. But this may appear that you are just stooping to playing his game. To avoid this actually being the case, your purpose must not only be higher, but your confidence must have a more solid foundation. We need something stronger than self-confidence. We need confidence in reality and our perceptions of it, enough to be able to stand even despite our own wavering doubts. Understanding empowers. Unearth the lies. What is their origin? What makes them so convincing? What damage has been done by them? How can you prevent believing them again?

Beliefs, particularly true ones, must be founded on reality. The evidence must point to the truth, by experience, observation, or explanation. Uncover truth because truth works. By implicitly trusting another fallible human being to direct you to truth (even if he may seem intent on helping you or claim love for you) is dangerous. It was likely that implicit trust that got you into bondage in the beginning. Instinct may be useful, but in the midst of manipulative tricks, it can also be misleading. Better to rest on facts and evidence, reasoning and results.

Illusions

With manipulation, the game is to create illusions—false portrayals that appear convincingly real. With them come a tremendous amount of talk and enthusiasm to prop them up and to entice followers with their appearance of uncommon greatness. Openness and sound reasoning are expertly avoided because lies do not stand testing. The pressure to accept the illusions must come along another line. It must be strong enough to lead individuals down paths they otherwise would not go. The illusionist is made powerful by molding minds to his purpose. But unless the audience knows it is a trick, an illusion is not impressive but deceptive. It is vital to know if what you see is real or not.

Rewriting reality as something else does not change reality. Regardless of how deeply embedded the illusions become, they are still empty. Covering up reality does not alter truth. Expertly concealing, justifying, reasoning, or otherwise convincing others of something different does not change what is. If claims are not founded on truth, even truth that is hidden, they will eventually fail. Failure proves them to be lies. The outcome reveals them as frauds. Though the senses can be expertly deceived for a time, the facts will tell. There is no security in what does not really exist. Neither will there be evidence to uphold it. So it is vital in the battles against manipulation to give a strong voice to reality, the visible reflection of truth.

Reality—as unimaginative, unpopular, or unpalatable as it may be—needs an advocate. It is safe, it is wise, and it is ultimately the soundest of investments. Take the stand firmly. Illusionists may claim that it is only your opinion and his opinion is elsewhere, but know that you are trying your best to cling to what is objectively right. Any opposing stance, however convincing, is not likely right. Not that you cannot err, but that there is a far greater chance that you are closer to truth if you are judging by reality, while he is likely only pressing for his own benefit. It is not so much a matter of putting more weight on one opinion over another anyway, but about building on what is true rather than elaborate fantasy. Moving to compromise with him moves you away from what is fair and best. Don't.

Evil Is

There are certain behaviors that are inherently wrong. There are motivations that are so completely un-empathetic that there is no humane explanation for them. There are harsh actions that may have a justification, but they fail to hold up against the grossly dehumanizing results. No amount of sympathy can explain away outright vileness. History's abominations are example enough: slavery, the Holocaust, human trafficking. And in this age of terrorism, we certainly have very present reminders of this far too often. Evil is very real.

Similar to degrees of murder, there are degrees of evil. There is evil by result, evil by intent, and evil by design. Manipulation falls into the second category: evil by intent. This means that it has an agenda that it is determined to achieve, and it will resort to evil if necessary to achieve it. It will not hesitate to violate the rights of others to gain something for itself. They may argue that it is not so bad as evil by design because its primary intention was not to harm—its end was not to wreak havoc, so it is not really so bad. Yet still, there also was no hesitation to harm, either. Invariably, it does result in harm. Innocent people have still been scarred by his actions, and he did nothing to prevent it. Nor is he likely learning from his mistakes. What he is doing is still evil. While the justice system does consider the degree of murder in sentencing the degree of punishment, there is still punishment. Evil must have its consequences.

In manipulation, wrong is often exalted as what is right and best. This is not a difficult line to blur, because evil itself is just a distortion of good. It is easy to be swayed by convincing appeals. An effective presentation touches our hearts, the person is likable, or we want him to be right—so we can be easily misled. It is no easy matter to sort through mixed truth. Therefore, it is crucial that the outcome of his claims is weighed. What evidence is there of goodness? What evidence is there of distortion? Look for the patterns before you draw any conclusions.

Characteristic of Wickedness	Characteristics of Goodness
Based on lies	Rests on reality
Creates increasing chaos	Promotes greater harmony
Generates fear	Lends hope
Establishes a bondage	Frees
Worsens with time	Improvements are obvious over time
Interferes with genuine good	Inspires more good
Usually justified as good or normal	Needs no self-justification

Once it gets a foothold, evil becomes unmanageable. It is foremostly irresponsible, often to the point where it becomes nearly impossible to reason with it. An appeal to the intellect is futile. It is also spreading, often drawing in innocent bystanders. And the negativity is so potent that the most gracious and loving methods fail to have any effect. At this point, the situation has gotten far beyond civil reform, no matter how insistent they are on their disguise of goodness. It is not about looking intently for the good to draw out anymore, but about facing the ugliness of the evil and defeating it. If all peaceful attempts at change fail, civility has reached its end. More aggressive methods for combating the unyielding wickedness are needed.

While bad can be transformed into better with a change in attitude or perspective, evil cannot. It must be handled with force and strength. If possible, appeal to a higher authority. The more power you can get to your punch, the more effective the recovery will be. But if you are the authority, you will need to rise to the occasion. Know the case well, and then act swiftly with resolve. Regardless of how cheery and optimistic we may try to be in the face of stifling oppression, evil will freely prevail until you engage it in battle. It needs to feel the force of justice.

So there are absolutes—points of black and white, good and evil. There are times when the issue is clear. There are moments when it is crucial to take a stand against a wrong. There is justice, and there is a means of weighing it. There are times to act on it with swiftness and resolve. A guilty verdict requires decisive action. And knowing when that time has come is vital to preventing tremendous disaster and suffering. Evil must be addressed as evil. There is no nice way to tackle it. Do what you need to do to fight it!

Justice and Mercy

In some sense, in wrestling against a manipulator, you have to become like him—staunch and unmoving. It feels dreadfully hypocritical, but it is the only way. He, expert that he is, may still maintain his pristine image through the stubborn stance, and you, unskilled, may be labeled the intolerant, hard-hearted one. It hurts and looks like the accusation is justified, but it is not. Standing firm is what is required. Just because you must take a battle stance does not mean that you are the aggressor, regardless of how the facts are reported.

The difference between being stubborn and being unyielding to boundary violations is very subtle. Stubbornness is driven by subjective wants, however disguised otherwise. Standing firm is driven by objective goodness, however misunderstood. Though the external behavior is very similar, the ultimate goal is completely different. And the method of dealing with the situation will often tell. Motivation matters. Stubbornness works for self-benefit. A manipulator wants more than is rightfully his, no matter how much he might justify it. He will compromise reason and integrity to gain control. The short-sighted nature of stubbornness will eventually tell to intelligent observers. It is just that enduring through the process of waiting for this awakening can be excruciating with the threats and uncertainty. Stand for justice anyway.

Justice looks for truth, makes a judgment based on the facts, and enacts the necessary consequences. It is indifferent to emotional dynamics. It looks for what is fair apart from personal bias. It looks to protect the natural rights of an individual. Though justice may consider motive in weighing the penalty's severity, there are still consequences. He must answer for his wrong behavior. Much of the doubt and confusion that manipulation stirs up must be set aside to make a judgment and be able to move forward. Even if imperfect or unpopular, justice needs to be honored and served.

Conversely, mercy is not a right, but an act of generosity. It should follow from trust—a confidence that this individual, though he may have failed, intends to change his course of action. The extent of justice that has been served was sufficient to correct the error. The shame has been faced and dealt with enough to move onto a better future. Mercy, rightly applied, is powerful. Mercy poorly applied can be disastrous.

Justice sees the deed; mercy sees the man. But they both must see clearly. Though one cannot exist without the other, each has its place. However unpopular, both boundaries and freedoms need to operate together in good relationships. A healthy life needs to have a foundation of both truth and love. Ancient cities needed walls, but they were not without gates, either. But when the very foundations are under attack and there clearly is no ground for peace, the hard virtues must rise to the occasion. Justice must prevail.

The Value of Objectivity

Through all the illusions, your one security is reality and your main access to that reality is objectivity. Often a circumstance transforms into a problem not because the effects are negative but because someone creates a fuss. It is the squeaky wheel that gets the most attention. That is why objectivity is so important in wrestling with manipulation. If subjectivity is given even an equal consideration, then a manipulator can make his voice seem so enormous that everything else is minor by comparison. Focus is drawn away from what is right, good, and best for everyone to what is the best way to quiet his piercing alarm. If there is a genuine concern, then addressing the issue will silence the squawking. If, however, the motivation is control, he will have a series of problems that are never satisfied. Addressing his issues ceases to be a matter of mercy and becomes enabling. We need to be able to see this objectively enough to judge this well.

While it is impossible to be perfectly objective, choosing to judge a situation by the facts has value. By looking at the situation as a scientific problem, often the steps toward a solution are not so unclear. With human interactions, subjectivity also has a place. What others think, believe, need, desire, feel, and hope for does matter. But when deception has invaded, the value of the subjective viewpoint is weakened. Your point-of-view may be disregarded or tainted by manipulation. His may be misrepresented or overpowering. Even those observing from the outside may fail to see the little details that make such a big difference. Opinions clearly are not a good place to rest your judgment. It is not about how people feel about the situation anymore but what is right overall. So there needs to be a strong focus on the impersonal perspective: reality.

It is important to face this reality. It is necessary to step out of the dynamics as far as possible. Even if you cannot instantly identify what is happening, you need to learn to trust a bit in your instinct of right and wrong—despite your best efforts to be fair and compassionate, despite how clearly you may see things from his perspective, despite the pressure of popular perception. Where there is manipulation, what is going on beneath the surface is too uncertain to be trusted. By tolerating the game, you only feed the illusion. Regardless of the degree of certainty in your snap judgments, it is wise to walk away from an artificial situation. Do not empower it by your silence and tolerance.

Objectivity seeks the truth. It often takes what is, tries to explain it through logical reasoning, and then tests the theory. The theory needs to be open to being proved wrong, and another idea is free to replace it. But once sufficient trials have confirmed an idea, it needs to be accepted as a fact. And this new discovery needs to be applied for any real progress to happen. Uncovering the truth ultimately leads to greater opportunity and security. It is a safeguard to face reality. But this also includes viewing yourself as objectively as possible. Look yourself squarely in the face, too. It may hurt at first, but it does far less damage in the end.

Integrity

People of goodwill generally come into a relationship with some fundamental expectations—equal dignity, mutual respect, a common objective for the common good. They expect that words are sincere and that your actions will agree with your intentions, by and large. In short, we believe that each of us is just trying to do his best with what he has to achieve something universally good. They expect judgments to be fair and consistent. Yet there is always respect, which is reflected in a willingness to learn, grow, and adjust for others. This openness to become better, to live by more universal and consistent principles, and to promote general well-being is integrity. There is a natural understanding that this is the way society functions best. While there may be secrets, there is no pretense, ulterior motives, intentional deceit, or habitual hypocrisy. What you see is largely what you get.

Integrity is vital for healthy relationships. It is a basis for trust. If someone does not have this behavioral standard, then it is all a guessing game where the line will be drawn. It is chaos and a very unstable environment. Manipulation, as a form of deceit, acts contrary to integrity. It looks to disguise reality as something else. The manipulator is driven to take what he wants while making it appear perfectly innocent. Because of this disparity between what he does and what he portrays, integrity erodes. Roles or situations may become compartmentalized. He can even begin to believe his own illusions are real. There are no longer strict governing principles over all of life, but ones that shift according to the situation. And he is master by furtively altering good judgment with coercion and confusion tactics.

The image he creates may be idealistic or superficially reasonable; outside appearances suggest that he is honestly trying to make the best of his world. Yet behind his veneer are very selfish and uninhibited intentions to gain an advantage. The actual motivation is disguised. And it is purposeful. By playing on our natural tendencies, he can sway situations to his advantage, undetected. Your natural, big-hearted reactions can draw you in deeper and deeper. Insisting on seeing the best in your manipulator feeds his control. Misplaced mercy can be a dangerous thing.

Yet there is a hidden untruth that will eventually surface. A shaky foundation will lead to the collapse of the building. The builder was not interested in creating a sound structure at all but only in filling his pockets. Relationships are similar. In the end, a sloppy foundation will not hold, and there will only be a big mess to clean up instead. Unfortunate to witness, painful to experience, but nevertheless inevitable.

You, however, must stand with integrity. Though being consistent, honest, and respectful may temporarily leave you vulnerable to even more manipulation, it must be endured. Learning to distinguish between what seems right and what is right is often strenuous. There will be doubt (likely intentionally introduced). By standing firmly on truth and insisting on reality, eventually the facts will surface to confirm your stand. Over time, the consistency of integrity is revealed, and the instability of manipulative tricks is unmasked. Standing firmly is ultimately the safest place in a world of shifting standards. But a firm stand does not mean passive inaction; it means playing shrewdly to reveal truth and being unmoved in that purpose.

Though you must play mind games, you must play by a different set of rules than your opponent. While his games are to promote confusion and misrepresent truth, yours must be to clarify understanding—your own first—and uncover the lies. On the surface, the strategies of the two sides do appear very much alike. You both play with shrewdness and calculation to undermine the other's purpose. But you must always remember that your purpose is truth. It must be grounded in reality, and your methods must always be upright. As tempting as it may be to lose your head and lash out in anger at the mean tricks, do not. It will only undermine your purpose in a hundred ways. Truth needs no manipulative tricks, just steady proclamation.

Levels of Trust

Your trust is one of the most precious gifts that you can give to another person. Beyond just a vote of confidence, it says that you are convinced enough of their abilities or character to place a piece of your well-being into their care. They are responsible for keeping you safe. But it also commits you. You will be expected to demonstrate some level of loyalty. You ought to support this person with your words or actions, because you believed he is good. Well-earned trust lends strength and security both ways.

As a gift, trust must be given with care. There must be good reason for you to believe that the person is trustworthy. Somehow, they have proven their abilities already so that you can rely on them, too. This might be in the form of an official certification or degree, recommendations from others, or your own personal observation. But there needs to be an external reason. Trust must be earned. There is a risk to trusting, but it should not be a foolish risk.

Because there are different things that you can entrust to people and different reasons for giving your trust, there are also levels of trust. You must understand how far you are willing to believe in them and how much of a risk you are willing to take based upon this belief.

- **Functional Trust:** There are times when you have no choice but to trust a person to follow through with responsible behavior. You cannot monitor everyone continually; it is entirely impractical. The only option is to trust. This is the type of confidence an automobile driver has in the builders of the bridge as he drives over it.

- **Trust in One's Judgment:** There are people whose judgments are trustworthy. People generally have areas of expertise, where their experience has taught them good practical choices and refined skill. These people earn your confidence in their ability, usually in one particular area. This is the type of trust a homeowner has in his certified electrician to rewire his home safely.

- **Trust in One's Word:** There are people whose word is trustworthy. They have shown that they are willing to make the extra effort to follow through with what they have said. They have been faithful to their promises before, and they are likely to be so again. This is the type of trust a couple might have for the neighbor boy to mow their lawn while they are away for the summer.

- **Trust in One's Character:** There are people who can be trusted nearly implicitly. Their priorities have been proven to be good by their actions. They understand what is ultimately most important and are committed to working toward that despite the cost to themselves. They stand firmly on what is most good and true. This is the trust we might place in an unsung hero, that his advice to us will be good and his actions in our behalf will be noble.

- **Trust with your Heart:** These are people you can trust because they love you personally and unconditionally. They genuinely have your best interest in mind, and if necessary, you trust them to put it before their own. Even if they make mistakes, you know that they will do everything in their power to set it right for you. This is the type of trust a small child might show toward his adoring parents.

How far you trust a person is your personal decision. You must be comfortable with the amount and type of evidence that you have collected yourself. And then the one who has been given your trust must prove to be faithful or that trust should be withdrawn. If you should not trust, do not trust. With manipulation, beware that it is not forced or obligated, either. If you notice this happening, it is a sure warning sign to withdraw your trust completely. Anyone who will try to get your devotion without earning it is certain to betray you. It is but the tip of the iceberg of deceit. Pull out and steer clear or it will easily destroy your peace, your happiness, and possibly even you!

Seeing Clearly Means Responsibility

When there has been a wrong conceived and embraced, eventually it surfaces. First, it only arises in the mind of man. Consciences sting. But if that twinge is ignored, it will feed into greater wrong beyond thought to intent and then to action. Left unchecked, this can become a lifestyle and then the root of evil is strong indeed. A mere idea then has worked its way to harming individuals, families, communities, or even societies, all quite possibly without remorse. All forms of slavery throughout history began as an idea to move toward something good by compromising (maybe just a little at first) the dignity of others. This leads to more and more compromise of souls until it is an epidemic. Built on indignity, the only cure of such perversion is then destruction. Clearly prevention is the greater solution.

The nature of manipulation makes it particularly difficult to detect in its early stages, however. By its very definition, it is meant to mislead with appearances of innocence. It wants you to buy into a lie and set aside a truth. Eventually, however, time will tell. Corrupt motivation cannot hide forever. Even if you are the only one who knows the truth. Whenever that time is, however belated in its revelation, it is the time for action. Despite all appearances, you *can* prevent further damage.

The longer you let a runaway train go without taking firm and drastic measures to stop it, the more damage it will do. Time only increases its momentum and the force required to stop it. Serious damage to all it is pulling, passengers included, is certain. If you cannot convince the engineer to put on the brakes and throwing up obstacles has failed, the time has come to cut off steam or to start disconnecting the train cars. Just waiting for a head-on collision is irresponsible and does no one any favors. If you are the one who knows what is happening, it is your responsibility to unmask it. Leaving this job undone will only make matters worse. He who sees a wrong, knows it is wrong—though he is not the one perpetrating it—and does nothing to stop it can be nearly as guilty as he who commits it. Do not become an accessory to his crimes! If you find there is a reason to rise up, then rise up you must. Develop a strategy and proceed with courage. There must be some concrete effort made to prevent the looming disaster. Do *enough* to stop it!

Accepting the Challenge

Once you have established that there is unquestionably an undertow of attack against dignity and the effects are ugly, the question becomes what to do about it. Choosing to fight it will require focused effort and sacrifice. There will be loss. And if the illusions are well orchestrated, there will be very little support. But lesser methods are generally ineffective, if not counterproductive. You must be prepared to rise up to do what needs to be done wholeheartedly and consistently if it is to be done well. Even amidst the persistent attacks against your confidence, you must stand firm. Doubts will arise, but remember reality. And do all that you can to secure what strength you can—but always justly.

Though unpleasant, bold deception needs to be shown for what it is. It is entirely appropriate to meet it with equally bold resistance and even repulsion. Manipulation needs to be met with shrewdness. Persuasion needs to be combated with reason. Isolated details need to be filled in with facts. The shadow shifting needs to be unmasked with the stronger light of truth. It can look very much like a tug-of-war, and as it is difficult to know who started it, you might look petty to onlookers. Generally, it is more prudent to just back down and let a petty matter go. But that is exactly what he is counting on you to do. This is no petty matter! When dignity, freedom, and truth are at stake, you must stand firm. Let go of what others may think of you, and keep reminding yourself of the real situation.

The battle is not so much against an individual, no matter how low he has stooped for selfish gain. It is against his lies. Lies that attack human dignity, respect, truth, and goodness. The most effective lies are those that have a good deal of truth mixed in. Manipulation expertly mixes. Ground yourself in what is right, down to the small details. Standing boldly for something that is fundamentally true often stirs up hidden fears in people, forcing them to face ugly truths buried deep within their hearts. Invariably, this wrenching of hearts excites fierce resistance. The more fundamental the lie, the more vehemently it will be promoted. The rising opposition confirms the value of your cause. Arm yourself with what is solid and true and then step forward boldly. There is great hope in courageously risking to proclaim truth. And in doing so, it helps others to face it, too. We cannot live an ideal until we have sorted through the real, so we must rise up. Accept the challenge.

8
RALLY YOUR RESOURCES

Once you have identified the source of the problem, have become convinced enough that it is worth fighting, and know enough of your enemy's tactics to be able to thwart them, then you need to get ready to act. It is time to rally your resources. Going into psychological warfare unprepared is certain defeat, so prepare for war.

While still not an absolute commitment to a full-fledged fight, this is a definitive action. The struggle has moved from theory into practice, and that can be intimidating. There is risk, uncertainty, and fear. The enemy is bold, confident, and well-established. Things are certain to get messy. So you need to do all that you can to secure your success. Your freedom is worth it. Justice needs you. Figure out what you have and start collecting what you will need. The better your resources, the more effectively you can fight.

Know Your Weaknesses, Know Your Strengths

If you are engaged in a battle, your enemy is studying you. He is determined to know your strengths—to avoid engaging you there—

and your weaknesses—to use to his advantage. It is important that you know what he knows, so know yourself. You too must understand your strengths. What will he avoid engaging because you will likely prove to be stronger? When will he avoid striking? Where, or with whom, would you be most alert to strike back against an attack? And likewise, when, where, and what conditions are you in your most vulnerable positions?

With manipulation, the game is very subtle. Where he is playing is subconscious and hidden, so you will need to understand yourself at that level also. This means that you will have to be frank with yourself in facing your fears, doubts, weaknesses, motivations, and devotions. Seriously ask such questions as:

- What stirs up your greatest fears?
(e.g. rejection, failure, pain, loneliness, loss)
- What situations make you uneasy?
(e.g. crowds, being cornered, focused attention, displayed anger)
- What lines of argument make you second-guess yourself?
(e.g. emotional, logical, intense, popular)
- When do you find you are weakest/least alert?
(e.g. mornings, after work, with your friends, when preoccupied)
- What motivates you the most?
(e.g. goals, success, pleasing people, duty, getting things right, self-satisfaction, praise)
- What do you value the most?
(e.g. your faith, family, possessions, reputation, power, dreams)

Once you have established where you are the most vulnerable, pay close attention to the dynamics. You will probably notice it is under those circumstances when you are most readily manipulated. Where you are most prone to move, he instinctively presses. And these are the points that need to be safeguarded more vigilantly.

Equally important to knowing your weaknesses is knowing your strengths. Weaknesses need to be guarded; strengths need to be utilized. If you can bring the battle around to be fought on your higher ground, you have a better chance of fending off the enemy. Play to your advantage, if only to counter him playing to your disadvantage.

- What skills do you have that influence people?

(e.g. proven integrity, written arguments, logical discourse)

- What form of communication do you find comes most easily?

(e.g. verbal, non-verbal, written notes, text, email)

- What gives you the most confidence when going into a difficult situation?

(e.g. preparation, affirmation, support, righteous indignation)

- How can you present yourself to show that you expect respect?

(e.g. dress, posture, grooming, scent)

You are defending truth, so you need to use your resources shrewdly. It has nothing to do with using your strength to gain the upper hand but with using your strengths to regain sanity. So do not hold back—he certainly is not. Choose to fight the battles when you are at an advantage, and stall when you are weakened. Your cause is so much higher and more vital than his. Begin fighting to win!

Find Support

Your most important resource after what is inside of you is your supporters. They are going to be there to listen, to understand, to help you see clearly despite the confusion, and to encourage you to keep going. They are precious, but they also must offer the right kind of support. People who do not believe in your judgment over and above their own limited perception of the situation, as well-meaning as they might be, are not going to be helpful. In fact, they will likely do far more harm than good. So your supporters need to be carefully vetted. People have to be convinced of the seriousness of the problem before they are willing to take a firm stand. They need to have followed a similar awakening to your own in becoming convinced of the problem's severity, either because they know what effect it has had on you or because they have been burned by the tricks, too. Assess their degree of loyalty and choose those who have the least doubt. The rest, leave alone.

The best way to determine the quality of the support you would get from an individual is by their response to your agony:

• **Suggesting changing your perspective:** Seeing from a different perspective is a legitimate place to begin. It helps develop a broader view of the situation and collect information. It is good to have vision and a positive attitude. But neither lose sight of the facts. It is a necessary preliminary, but know that in dealing with uprooting deceit, you have long since exhausted its usefulness. Do not embrace this type of help.

• **Offering explanations or mediation:** A safe place to proceed is by trying to understand. Often if we can understand a problem, it is easier to accept it or master it. The neighbor is upset at our music because he works night shifts. Once we understand, we are more eager to oblige and the trouble dissolves. Fine—if the problem is simple, and you are dealing with a reasonable person. People may guide you this way, but if you are entangled in any real manipulation, you likely have been far too empathetic with your manipulator already. Do not lose sight of truth and justice in your effort to find peace! Decline their offers.

• **Extending sympathy:** This is the first sign of understanding the real threat to dignity. Even if people feel helpless to be helpful, they can at least be sympathetic. A listening ear and a compassionate heart are rare finds. Often these treasures are only found in those who have known indescribable grief themselves.

• **Giving relief:** Sympathy in action. This takes the initiative to do something, however small, to give the sufferer a moment of relief and a sweet taste at dignity. It is a vote of confidence and support, which often far outweighs any tangible good they actually do.

• **Equipping:** This is the act of supplying the suffer with the necessary tools to actively combat the struggle. It may be in the form of practical provision, education, confidence, or strategy, but its purpose is to empower. If someone else has been there before, they know what you are fighting far better than words can describe. They can offer strong support.

• **Advocating:** These are the rare souls who are willing to speak up against your particular injustice, strategically to those in power. Even if they are only hired, they are fighting the fight of the mind and being a voice for the voiceless. It is a strong vote of support, not only for you but also for the cause at large.

• **Offering refuge/escape:** These are the bold players who will defy convention to right an injustice. At great personal risk, they are willing to invest their own resources to rectify the wrong—by defiance, if necessary. They believe in you enough to suffer personal loss themselves. They help bear the expense—be it time, money, inconvenience, or disgrace—they are in the trenches fighting with you.

Judge the commitment level. As desperately as you might need support, do not compromise your purpose. Not that you should blame most of them for taking a weaker stance, but know that they will be of no benefit to you. Politely pass on their offers. Getting them involved will only cloud the issue more—which is only to the manipulator's advantage. You choose who is good for *you*.

Turn to family first, and then trusted old friends. Anyone who has known you well before you got tangled in the manipulation would be a good place to look. If you managed to develop any friendships that were kept completely separate from your manipulator, they could also be a good support. And lastly, your fellow sufferers who are or have been trapped in the same situation, be it siblings, coworkers, or grown children. If they are in it, too—bond! But if you have to go through the tedious process of explaining the complex dynamics and subtle tricks to convince someone, they are not going to support you. Focus elsewhere. It is better to go through the fight with a few loyal comrades than leaning on those with divided loyalties who will end in betraying you, even ignorantly.

Collect Evidence

Collect what evidence you do have to support your claims. There probably will not be much, but anything is better than nothing. It most often is in the form of notes from third parties, but it could also be photos, financial records, or medical documents. You may not need it to win a court case (hopefully), but it might help convince key people or even help convince yourself. Dig up what you can and have it ready.

It is also helpful to collect your experiences. Write them down. In most cases, you are your own greatest evidence. Your distress is probably more obvious than you realize; you just need to put it into context. Document incidences, present and past, that illustrate what has been happening behind closed doors. With manipulation, it will be impossible for you to remember everything, but do highlight some. Just describe what happened, without emotionalism, and how it represents a pattern of behavior. If you need it, it will be there. In the meantime, thinking this through can help clarify your stance in your own mind: his treatment of you *is* shameful.

Carve Out a Haven

You need a place of refuge, someplace where you can be yourself and catch your breath before the next round. It should be a place where your manipulator cannot or will not go. Here you can keep your notes, your evidence, your emergency resources. Here you can post reminders of who you are, strategies for fighting, and vision for a better tomorrow. It is a place to let go of the strain briefly, a place where you can be yourself without threat. It is a place of grounding in reality amidst the shifting illusions. And you need it.

Even if you do not have a physical place, carve a time-out with a walk, a drive, a locked bathroom. Glean sanity from normal people—even strangers in public. Grab at happiness when the lurking shadow is not watching. A physical haven is best, but at the very least, create a mental one. You may have one already because it is also essential for enduring continual pressure, but it will become even more important in the fight. With an increase in tension, there will be an increase in the intensity of emotion. You will need a place of privacy where you will be able to think more clearly. There needs to be a safe place for you to process the confusion and the emotions, a place where it is possible to scream, cry, or rant without being observed. (You do not need accusations of being unstable on top of *everything* else!) A place of refuge where, for at least a bit, you will not be judged or betrayed.

Secure Your Finances

Depending on what level of freedom you hope to achieve, this may or may not be a significant consideration. If losing your job might be a real possibility, make sure you have enough saved to hold you over until the next one comes along. If there is a chance you will have to leave your home, make sure you have a plan for how to pay for somewhere else. If attorneys or counselors are necessary, have the resources to cover them. Once battles are drawn out from the shadows, the chaos can become intense, and nothing is sacred. You need a nest egg. Start a secret stash and research what other financial resources might become available to you, if necessary.

Have an Emergency Plan

Resistance to deeply embedded lies can excite violent reactions. Once the battle commences, things can get ugly. Generally, with manipulation, you can back down the intensity a bit simply by complying, but *only* to buy yourself some time. If there are hints that things could get dangerous, you need to have a plan of escape. Whatever you hoped to achieve through the battle, your life is more valuable. If you are in physical danger, scrap the plan and get out! Hang your reputation and take the steps. Diplomacy, courtesy, respecting decisions and property—all that might have to be set aside to save a life. Do it. If others are not at risk, discard their opinions (all of them)—know that wisdom will be shown right by her actions. Just go! The more warning you have, the more you can get out with dignity and security; but if that fails, get out without them.

Think about where you will go and how you would get there. Have a list of what to pack: birth certificates, clothes, toiletries, contact numbers, cash, blankets, medications, legal documents. Make a plan of how to ease the news to any children that might have to come with you or anyone you must leave behind. Turn off all location services. Be mindful of covering your tracks. You have been psychologically hunted already, so you probably know how to avoid some detection. But if it becomes dangerous, a plan can keep you focused and safe. Regardless of what it implies, make one. And if you need to use it, go!

Your resources are important to have, even if you do not ever need to use them. They help to give you courage, knowing there is something more substantial behind you than just your gut. You have some things that can reaffirm your claims and some people who are willing to walk beside you and cover your back. You have some resources to turn to when all else seems to be lost. These are also the reminders that you will need to help you get back up when you fall or begin to doubt the value of your cause. They help to lend you confidence. And they are where you can turn if the situation turns on you.

9
TAKING ACTION

ENGAGING THE BATTLE begins by pushing back, by offering resistance. You may have tried this before, but now you are better prepared when things begin to escalate. You know it is a game, so you do not have to put up with the nonsense. You know there are tricks, so your suspicions are aroused. You know what it is really about, so you are not so easily distracted from the real issue. You have begun to counter the isolation and division with good support. You anticipate the pressure, so you can resist persuasion and coercion. You are equipped. Now it is just a matter of doing it.

Fighting for Freedom

Your battle against control is for freedom. Piece by piece, you need to focus on reclaiming it. Where exactly your battle lies, however, depends upon how much freedom you already have and how much you hope to gain. Freedoms and the strength to protect them build on each other, however. You need to have freedom of thought before you could ever hope to achieve financial freedom. So determine where you are and where you would like to be. Build up from the basic ones to those that will require more resources and planning. The strategies are similar because it is all about breaking bondage, but where you must take your bold moves will differ. Determine where you need to begin your fight.

The Battle for Freedom at Various Levels

Mental Independence

If an invasion has been made in the mind and emotions, then the most strategic plan is to battle in the mind. The first step to independence must be there. How you think will affect your choices in every other area of your life. The mind is a powerful tool. If yours has been invaded, it is vital to regain that ground first. He who has mastered your mind, even partially, has mastered you. If you cannot be free to direct your own thoughts, you are indeed a prisoner. And this is exactly what manipulation wants. Once the mind is largely molded, the rest is not so hard to control. So think, think, think!

Mental independence is achieved when you are able to step back from a situation and view it from your own personal perspective. It gives preference to *your* knowledge, *your* experience, and *your* judgment. It may take others' opinions into account when considering what is best or right, but it is not dominated by them. It steps back to judge for itself, with as much honesty and objectivity as it can. If necessary, it is willing to look deeper into the matter. And if mature, it is prepared to take responsibility for whatever steps it chooses to take.

Signs of mental bondage include tolerating being told what you think (even indirectly), evaluating your choice predominately on your manipulator's opinions, or choosing based on some other overly idealized principle. In severe cases, you may not even know how to see from your own perspective because you are so accustomed to seeing from his. To overcome this, you need to recognize that you are being overshadowed. The more you understand how this is happening—be it by fear or urgency or brainwashing techniques—

the better you will be equipped to pull away. In all cases, though, buying time is of the essence. When you are pressed for a decision, pull away from the pressures as far as you are able; view it first as an objective bystander might see it. Decide based on what seems right or wise. Express your conclusions with confidence and see where it leads, despite the nagging doubts. Do not apologize for your thoughts—see if they prove to be right first. You are on the road to a higher good. With time, you will be able to see more naturally from your own perspective, knowing your own mind, opinions, and proven principles without the tangling doubts. In the meantime, fight for it. With mental freedom comes clarity. And seeing clearly will give you the strength to keep going on.

Emotional Independence

Being emotionally free implies that you feel what you naturally would feel. Instead of feeling what you have been led to feel, you can come to know your emotions as your own. The tactics that play off of your emotions—guilt trips, pity play, intimidation-—fail to hold as much sway. What you want is not to be dictated by your manipulator but by your own judgment and experience. You are free to feel what you normally would despite the manipulation, without fear. If you are conditioned to identifying with the emotions of your manipulator (knowing what he feels so well that those emotions become part of your own, if only to predict and protect yourself), you need to be free of that as well. It is not that you should become indifferent, but that you can keep the emotional influence of others in good check. It is not an insensitivity, but a localized desensitivity. Not that you do not care, for you most certainly do, but that you will not be mastered just because you *do* care. Emotions are meant to be a gauge of your own well-being, not strings to master you.

Gaining emotional independence can be heart-wrenching. Instead of relying on your internal senses, you will have to rely heavily on your intellect. That is why it is vital to achieve solid mental independence first. You have to be firmly convinced of what is best in order to defy the powerful pull toward easing the emotional discomfort. Strong personalities can effortlessly dominate the emotional climate. Your goal is to avoid being significantly impacted by the atmosphere and step out enough to evaluate what is actually happening despite the pull. You must know what is right to do over and above what feels right at the time. You must believe in what you are stepping out to do despite the ache and longing for a different way.

Of course, overriding all emotions is dangerous. Love and rational fear need to be kept intact to a large extent. Guilt, pity, and shame, however, might have to be overridden. The guilt that rushes in through this process might feel overwhelming. The justifications to listen to the guilty accusations might seem normal. You have been conditioned by mistreatment, and those familiar emotions can feel so natural, but they are not. This is an intense battle because it is within yourself. It is between the foreign pressures that have been expertly planted there and your much-neglected genuine self. To give the natural the extra strength it needs to eventually overcome requires a determination to proceed forward with or without the sense that what you are doing is best. In this stage, you are faced with a dilemma between what feels right and what is right, instinct versus intellect. It is a clash of realities—one from your senses, the other from the facts. Intellectually, absolutely you must believe it. Emotionally, however, your heart (conditioned by deceit and fear) may not agree and will have to be disregarded for a time.

This is destabilizing. It will feel like the ultimate self-betrayal, but it is not! It is similar to facing a risky surgery when the discomfort is still not completely unbearable. Yes, the pain can be avoided just now, but at what ultimate cost? Suffering must be chosen when you know the alternative is worse. It will take great courage and a bold disregard of self-doubt. Yet unlike other such difficult choices, gaining emotional independence is not a one-time decision. You will not have to go against your instinct just once, but continually for a time. And it is agony.

It all can be very disorienting. It may be difficult to judge what is right and wrong anymore. What you must do—fight the pressure—will feel impossible and traitorous; what you may want to do—let it pass and appease—would be the easier route. Of course it seems safer to avoid a battle that will likely end in certain defeat, at first. That is exactly why manipulation has such a strong hold in the first place. You are not engaged in a single battle, however; this is a prolonged war. Focus on the vision. In warfare, with time and experience, you will see results. Until then, this is a tremendous step of faith into a dark unknown. It is wise to get quality support.

Knowing the origin of the negative emotions is key to achieving independence. Naturally, we might assume that our emotions are our own because they arise from the core of our being. But if this subconscious has been unknowingly invaded, your emotions may not be an accurate reflection of you at all. If you cannot relieve the pressure, you at least can begin to lessen its impact. Step by painful step, rise above the dynamics enough to understand so that you no longer have to be mastered by the games. They are not based on truth and do not have your best interest at heart. Fight for your best. Coming to your senses is a glorious release and opens up a world of fresh hope.

Spiritual Independence

Gaining spiritual independence means that you are free to hold your own beliefs and to be with those who share them. As a mature adult, being told what you are to believe, how you must worship, or where you must attend church are all examples of spiritual oppression. Though it is common for religions to exert pressure, not only on their members but on outsiders as well, insisting theirs is the only "right" method, you must ultimately weigh truth for yourself. You personally are going to be held responsible for what you stand for. Be sure that you have weighed the claims by the fruits and not by the claims alone. Truth stands testing. We cannot naively believe all that we are told. There must be evidence. While faith is a journey with twists and turns, like most things in life, yours must not be too forcefully directed by another. If you are not free to live your faith as a journey toward truth but instead are being pressured to settle on some pre-defined dogmas, you may be in spiritual bondage. Perhaps you will eventually find the same claims to be universally right, but you must find that yourself.

Gaining a spiritual independence involves making your beliefs your own. To some extent, you can find this liberty of belief in your own mind. But rich faith is indeed a corporate journey, so this should not be done in complete independence and isolation, if possible. Often it is done best by exploring ideas with others in a safe environment. But if the quest is for truth, those ideas must also be tested. You must have the freedom to question, to doubt, to test, and to draw your own conclusions. There must be a freedom to reasonably choose where, when, how, and with whom to discover what is ultimately true and lasting. Find a way to carve a niche for this. History is rife with those who had to go underground to keep their faith. But your quest for truth should not be dictated by another. Find your freedom there, too.

Social Independence

You must have the freedom to choose your own friends and how you will spend your free time. You need to be reminded what normal feels like and how reasonable people act. You need to be around people who value you, where you can feel some dignity and joy. While obligations might press you into less desirable social environments, you must have the time and resources to choose for yourself *sometimes*. Your pleasurable human interactions cannot be continually compromised without damage. You will grow dull without them. Manipulation knows this, and that is why isolating you from those types of people is so important to him. Make the opposite important to you.

Few responsibilities are more important than keeping your sanity. The people that are key to your life, those who uphold your identity and worth, need to have regular contact with you. They are the ones who support you and lend you strength. They are the ones who reaffirm or refine your perspective in a safe environment. Get around people you can trust, who care about you personally, who will fight for your interests when you no longer have the strength. This is especially important if you are subjected to a continual barrage of illusions and distortions. You need help seeing through the fog.

You need to be there for them also. Others are missing out on the pleasures of your company when you are not there. Community is stronger in unity, and that requires a consistent time investment. Be with people who will build into you. And build into people who appreciate your investments into them. It is far more important than it might seem.

Often gaining social independence requires delegating responsibility to others—preferably back to those who have unreasonably delegated them to you. Do so. If the chaos factor must increase for a time so that you can reach some social stability, let it. Social independence is revitalizing. It can boost confidence more quickly in the midst of oppression than anything else; it is a breath of hope to those in bondage. And in the end, the return on the investment will be well worth the loss.

Financial Independence

Financial bondage means that you do not have the freedom to obtain the resources you believe are important. Somehow money is tightly controlled, and your voice of how it should be spent for the best is disregarded. This can leave you scrambling, weakened, or ashamed. You cannot invest into what you believe in because you have almost nothing. You cannot move beyond to make a difference or make progress without resources. Any bold venture toward tangible freedom is going to require capital.

As far as possible—by separating finances, changing jobs, finding a job—become master of your own money. Financial independence is the most widely respected freedom. It is universally understood and establishes almost an instant power. The more you are able to support yourself and your choices, the more you are able to establish yourself as separate. Even if you cannot ever fully achieve physical independence, financial independence may be the final step you need to be completely free. It is the crudely practical step on your road to liberty, but it also demands a great deal of support. It might require you to use the full scope of your other newly acquired freedoms to achieve it also. Promoting yourself to get a new job or finding the courage to reject a financial gift may be the ultimate test on this journey.

It will require shrewdness, sound judgment, some risk, and a good dose of self-confidence. If you have found the strength to procure the other freedoms, though, you are capable of this step also. But do not skimp on preparation, and do not rush yourself. You must not go forward before you are properly prepared or you may end up losing much of what you have fought to gain so far. Proceed with caution, but by all means—proceed! Expand your skill set, revamp you resume, start making contacts, fill out applications. Setbacks are not failures. Keep trying. And with this independence comes a newfound respect from others, which can be powerful in itself.

Physical Independence

Creating physical distance is a clear establishment of boundaries. Being away from the situation, especially one that includes high pressure, is clearly beneficial. It provides a more permanent refuge where you can regain a grasp on reality and be strengthened for the next encounter. It helps to create a place where there is not such a strain to be vigilant in the midst of deceit. It gives you a mastery of your own space—you can determine who is permitted into your home. And there are physical locks to reinforce your stance. Going away is a definite sign of cutting off. The more unreachable you are, the less you can be controlled. Physical independence changes the pressure points. Instead of underlying mental pressure, there is practical pressure of providing for yourself and navigating the world alone. Suddenly, you find yourself faced with managing your own possessions and responsibilities, and that without a fight. As novel and perhaps awkward as it may feel at first, welcome the liberty.

Physical independence is a tremendous step. Depending on how entrenched your life is with your manipulator, it may require an enormous amount of risk and sacrifice. You will have to venture into stepping where you never expected to step, learn new skills, grieve over loss of the familiar on multiple levels, and take the opportunities to redefine yourself. It will require shrewdness and creativity. Likely the fight will become more vicious because this is the final battle of the war. Be fully prepared. If you fail now, it will be harder to succeed later.

All of these steps, in their own way, feel very awkward or terrifying at first. Often there will be heated objections to your new boundaries. Your independence is a severe threat to his security, and strong manipulators will ensure that you suffer the full force of discomfort for taking it. So it can feel wrong. It creates havoc, internally and externally. But ultimate order can only be achieved by first creating a temporary mess. Before you can organize a very cluttered closet, it is best to take it all out. The mess looks far bigger than when you started, but with diligence, order inside and out will be restored.

Manipulation is about control. If it feels that control is being threatened by your unmasking, it will seek to regain it in other ways. This often means a shift in the type of manipulation. Be prepared for new tricks. They will probably grow more dramatic, intense, and involved. Do not be drawn in—they are probably still tricks. So do the research and draw reasonable conclusions. Keep pressing to uncover the truth. But once manipulative tricks are exhausted and the game is not working so well anymore, he might begin to resort to more extreme measures. Veiled threats can become real ones. Lies can become more pointed and crueler. Innocent people can be drawn in and punished for your defiance. Your resources might be cut off or your safety threatened. Your fears of what you might awaken by resisting could become a reality. That is why it is so important that you have a clear understanding, strong support system, and resources to fall back upon. You might have to resort to extreme measures just to avoid imminent disaster. As unpleasant as this is, it might be necessary. If things grow intense, begin to turn your attention to your emergency plan. Start to iron out the details. Fortunately, the escalation of events does not come without warning signs, so heed them and begin to prepare.

Survival Strategies

In battle, the purpose is two-fold: achieving the ultimate goal and survival until then. The ultimate goal under unreasonable control is complete independence. The control needs to be broken. Unfortunately, that is not always in your power to perfectly achieve, and what you can do can be a lengthy process. So clearly the immediate problems also need attention. Gladly, the steps to coping do contribute to the solution, but victory is not often clear. You need smaller victories to mark progress, and until the rescue, there needs to be some relief. Where independence is impossible or yet to be realized, there are coping strategies.

Short of completely avoiding the manipulator, the initial strategy for dodging manipulation is to stay one step ahead of the game. Prevent it. If you can predict what is coming, you are generally able to head off the trouble beforehand. But this requires a tremendous amount of insight and energy. It leaves you absorbed and exhausted much of the time. Though you are less of a victim, it still leaves you in a kind of bondage to the control. And if perchance you do fail to foresee the crisis, more blame often falls on your poor predicting ability than on the aggressor's affront. But even when you did have enough insight to prevent it, you are still weakened, and he is still fresh for a new angle of attack.

Because of this, the most effective strategy for dealing with manipulation is letting it happen and stepping aside to allow the consequences to follow. The difficult part is mentally untangling your involvement from the situation. Pulling emotionally away from the drama is no easy task. Despite your contribution to the situation being somehow less than perfection, you should not rush in to try to make things better. You are not responsible for correcting or soothing the bad effects of his behavior. In most cases, you should not even be required to endure them. Be unaffected and walk away. (Easier said than done...)

Apply Vigilance

In an ideal world, there is no deceit and no need for vigilance. If the manipulator can convince you to buy into the ideal, where there is perfect trust (without him having to earn it), then he is free. He can conjure distortions without hindrance. Tricks are not part of the ideal, so they do not exist. Or so goes the argument; and then you will find yourself juggling a very odd version of reality.

If you are regularly being manipulated, this simplistic trust must be abandoned. You cannot trust someone who has proven to be untrustworthy. This includes refusing to give him the benefit of the doubt (which is just excusing his behavior). It means abandoning hope for some miraculous revelation and change, and it means being very wary of making any compromise with him at all. You cannot afford to be drawn naively into deceit while all the warning signs are there.

Be watchful and alert. If you notice your sense of shame or anger aroused, that is a good sign that you are being had. Hold your tongue and step out of the moment. Know the game and be prepared to defy it. Be vigilant. Ignore the implications of what he is saying and ask yourself what he is doing. The sooner you can foresee where the tricks are going, the sooner you can halt them. Even if you cannot predict them, being aware of the manipulation and having a plan of counterattack in place is vital. And then boldly act on it. But do not let being alert consume you, either. Ceaseless vigilance is completely exhausting. Just be prepared as best you can, and do not believe the lie that "you should have seen it coming." In a just society, there should not be manipulative tricks at all. But since there are, boldly act against them as quickly as possible.

Vigilance is not only alertness and focused attention; it is also a keenness of mind that grows as it learns. It comes to recognize patterns and to identify signals. It knows what the enemy is likely to do. It is not afraid to face facts and interpret them from past experience. It knows when to look, where to look, and what to do next. It uses its best training and preparation to sound an alert when there is a threat. And it will boldly appeal to authority or call for reinforcements.

Establish Boundaries

Once you have identified the common points of attack (generally your most vulnerable ones), it is wise to protect. While a defense is important when a crisis comes, building a hedge of protection is a much sounder investment. Boundaries, once in place, are automatic. They do not necessarily require any adjustment for new situations or continual strategizing. They do not need exertion of manpower. They, like walls, once established and maintained, simply exist and are effective that way. They are an invaluable first line of defense. And when they are compromised, defeat is often not far behind.

Physical boundaries are obvious. They establish where objects belong and where they are kept safe. If they are not concrete, often they are somehow labeled—signposts, lines, laws, or rules. They are meant to be understood and respected. When they are not, steps are taken to administer consequences. Similarly, there needs to be personal boundaries, limits that are not to be exceeded. If they are not naturally understood, efforts need to be made to establish them. And enforce them.

Boundaries in relationships are often more indistinct than other types of boundaries, which makes knowing when they have been crossed difficult to identify. But boundaries still must exist. We are each distinct individuals who need safety from invasion. Though what constitutes safety and invasion might vary significantly by the individual and the relationship, whatever boundaries you have created for yourself need to be respected. You need to know that you have a haven. But you are also responsible for creating and protecting that haven. Only you can know when you feel threatened, and you must be prepared to resist the affront, however unintentional it may be. Your boundaries are your safety. Build them based on your trust.

Unfortunately, you have to draw a broader and thicker line around those who have proven to take advantage of you. Boundary violations *require* you to offer resistance. Practically, it may include several shifts in behavior:

- Firmer no's
- Allowing less ground for rousing your suspicions
- Strict adherence to agreed policy
- No display of doubt
- Limiting time, attention, and resources

But remember that with manipulators, sloppy boundaries are no boundaries at all. So you *must* be firm. These steps may be accused of being harsh, unyielding, cruel, rude, unreasonable, unfair, or crazy, but it is only because they are purposely discounting the behaviors that drove you to such extremes. If they were not pushing the boundaries, you would have no need to enforce them so strongly.

(These accusations, in fact, are a sure sign that the boundaries are desperately needed.) Boundaries are not meant to protect selfish ambition or shameful truths, though people can use them that way. They are to protect justice, sanity, peace, and dignity. Use them well.

When learning to create boundaries, you must regain your trust in your gut. Even if you cannot immediately pinpoint the particular manipulation technique, certainly there is a twinge of hesitancy or doubt. At first, you may just need to go with it, especially if it is with someone who has used you frequently before. Even if it will cause tension or pain, draw a firm boundary. It may be sloppy, it may be off target, and it may be harsh. The necessary first step is to get some kind of a barrier up, no matter how makeshift. Right now, the issue is not perfection but getting stronger to fight. In time, you will become better at distinguishing where boundaries are necessary. For now, err on the side of safety—yours. It is far easier to back down later than to regain lost ground. Defend your walls.

> Greta recently moved to a new country for her new position. As she is very unattached, her coworkers frequently ask her to take their holiday shifts for them. Unfamiliar with the culture, she regularly obliges. But then she finds she is missing out on many cultural experiences, which was one of her main reasons for immigrating. Though she had no specific plans, she refuses to take the Christmas shift. Sitting alone in her apartment that day, listening to carols on the radio, she does feel guilty. Perhaps she could have spent her time more nobly working for Harriet...

There will be mistakes; learn from them and move on.

Expect Responsibility

With freedoms come responsibilities. They are a package deal. We must do our part to maintain order so that we all can enjoy more freedom. A driver's license opens up the world, but you must be responsible in order to earn *and* keep that privilege. The consequences of failed responsibility are loss of privilege; the freedoms and benefits you once enjoyed can and will be adjusted as necessary. It is the way of justice. The demands might seem steep, but they are necessary.

By expecting responsibility, you are establishing a standard and, by implication, consequences for failing to meet that standard. If this policy is new, it will be resisted. Those who have been enjoying too much privilege at the expense of someone else will balk. It is comfortable to be pampered, and resistance is easier than being responsible. But you must still insist. And when responsibility is dropped, natural consequences should follow. It must cost the irresponsible one some personal benefit. Unfortunately, sometimes you are going to be the one that must enforce it.

With its standard setting and consequence enforcement, demanding responsibility can look a lot like control. There is a pressure to get the other to move. It does make the other option of not changing more unpleasant. There is a stern demand without compromise. On the surface, it can look hypocritical, and you will likely be viciously accused of control yourself. But creating pressure is different from refusing to relieve it. Though the method is nearly identical, the difference is in the purpose. If the pressure is for some personal benefit, irrespective of the dignity of another, it is control. If it is for greater order for all, it is expecting responsibility. The difference is subtle, so it is an easy thing for him to claim a natural consequence is your vengeance. It is just a matter of shifting the cause.

Cadence and Claude are twin teens who share a vehicle. Cadence tends to run the tank to empty each time she takes it out, so Claude insists she keep it at least a quarter full. Cadence is annoyed and denies she does that, and she accuses Claude of being overbearing and demanding special treatment.

If the consequences are emotional, the difference is even more difficult to recognize. It is hard enough to determine if emotions are willful or natural, justified or unjustified, even when they are your own.

Mark's Aunt Hattie has been talking badly about his fiancée, Jana, ever since she met her. Mark is hurt by this, and though he does not completely understand why, he is repulsed by Hattie's pretense to Jana's face. So Mark refuses to show anything but a cool respect to Hattie. Hattie is enraged and claims that Mark is trying to pressure her into approving of Jana by cutting her off from his affections. Mark is taken aback by the accusations and wonders if there is some truth to them.

Look beyond the words themselves to see their purpose. If the hurt they cause does no real good, then it was meant merely to hurt you. If it does press toward some greater peace and justice, then it ought to be considered, *later*. Do not let the bold counterattack dissuade you from upholding your boundary. You need to be the one to judge when and how it should be let down—and then only on very solid ground of proven character.

Natural withdrawal can look like withdrawal to control. Establishing firm boundaries can look like trying to confine others. Appealing to authority can look like intimidation. Allowing consequences can look like enacting unjust punishment. And you can be assured, a talented manipulator will make your steps look just that way. Be prepared. It is important that you stand firm anyway. Keep reminding yourself of the real situation.

The fierce opposition is why it is so important that you step out wisely. Do not interfere with his freedom, rights, resources, or dignity. These are the essential ingredients of humanity, and if you expect yours to be respected, you must respect his. You must play fair, even when he does not. If you do not, you will be in grave danger of becoming controlling also. Stick to integrity, even if the lies about you sound very much like the truth you are telling of him. Your perspective still needs to be defended, regardless of how much you doubt being believed. As much as it might feel like a disadvantage, fight the temptation to stoop to his level. But that does not mean that you cannot play smart and play to win.

Though it may be awkward and unpleasant, there is generally a way to achieve justice without violating dignity. The choices are not strictly between destroying and being destroyed. The third option of unwavering defense, though requiring tremendous stamina, is the best option. Hold the fort without making an aggressive attack. While you should not interfere with his humanity, neither should you interfere with his responsibilities. Expecting your freedoms, rights, resources, and dignity to be respected also is not being controlling. It is not even being unreasonable. It is basic justice. And sometimes that justice requires a fight to uphold. Violations of justice have consequences. Stand for what is right.

Defer the Blame

If you begin to apply any of these tactics, from achieving some sort of independence to expecting responsibility, there will be resistance. Manipulation does not like people interfering with its system. It wants to be master and master alone, so even your coping strategies are threatening. And that can arouse a host of counterattacks. These are usually just more intense forms of the same manipulation techniques—trying to play off of your guilt, pity, shame, pride, or fear. But when you may already be struggling with weakness and doubt, they can be very unsettling. Keep digging up truth and cling to vigilance, boundaries, and redistributing responsibility. But how to sort through the shame?

Though difficult to master, an important key for dealing with manipulation is blame deference. Instead of owning the shame that has been dumped onto you, you simply leave it unaddressed. Just because you can take (and likely have taken) responsibility for the problem, it does not mean that you should. If the shame is not your own, you can do nothing with it—and you should not. You should not take ownership of the shame and blame from unreasonable accusations. Instead of arguing or defending yourself, though, which just plays into manipulation, it is often wiser to just brain dump. If there is garbage flying at you, it is not going to benefit anyone if you swallow it. Let it fall where it lies. It is not worth any attention. Metaphorically, you should just stick your fingers in your ears. Be determined not to let it bother you. Let him rant because it is really not you who is the problem.

> *Mr. Harvey is a junior vice president of his company. After every executive meeting that he must attend, he calls Zane, his manager, into his office. Zane is then required to sit there and listen to Mr. Harvey rant and explain why Zane is the cause of all Mr. Harvey's job troubles. By implication, he is degraded as being incompetent, unreliable, dimwitted, and sometimes malevolent. As Mr. Harvey's eloquence and presence is imposing, Zane was crushed by these floods of rebuke at first. Then he learned. Though still required to endure these lecture sessions, Zane now dismisses the ugly blame that gets dumped on him there. Instead, he focuses his mind on other things: watching Mr. Harvey's eyes bulge, observing the contour of his face, counting the number of words in each of his sentences, or studying the carpet pattern.*

The idea of deferring blame is that you understand the dynamics well enough to know that something deeper is going on than what you can influence. Though there may be much blame—spoken with sweetness or in anger—if it is not deserved, do not allow it to transform into shame. Once you internalize it, it can wreak havoc.

Though nearly impossible to do perfectly, leave the words to fall unheeded. As convincing as he may make it sound, it is not about you at all. Do not be bothered by his accusations. They are not spoken to reach truth but to distract from it. Do not take them in. The ugliness is only a symptom of a deeper problem that has nothing to do with you. While "shutting down" might seem cold, it is a natural, reasonable, and prudent response to excessive negativity. Let him stoop to low measures, but you make it your ambition to walk away unaffected. It is not rude; it is shrewd.

Relax In Between

It is important that you conserve your strength and sanity by embracing the opportunities to relax between the encounters. When the pressure is off, use your time to richly delve into the things that mean the most to you. Invest in the people you love (and who will love you in return), participate in the activities that bring you pleasure, carve a time of happiness and peace in an otherwise chaotic world. Though it may appear that this is not helping to solve your overwhelming problem, it is most important. You need a firm grasp on your own identity simply because it is being so viciously undermined. Remember who you are and what happiness actually means. It is your lifeline to reality. Relish the relief.

Carve Out Time to Think

After an underhanded offense, you need time alone to process the situation. For the sake of justice, you must honestly and regularly assess the situation and make fair judgments. Especially when you are forced to rely a bit heavily on your gut reactions in order to counter aggressive attacks, it is even more important that you consider the validity of your reactive-responses. Having time to process is essential. Use it to:

• Unscramble the situation
• View the dynamics more objectively

- Evaluate the legitimacy of the emotions—on both sides
- Consider other possible explanations
- Notice the patterns of behavior
- Weigh the evidence
- Strategize
- Erect boundaries

Along with clearing your perspective and setting a course of action, time also allows you to ache, mourn, grieve, rage, rant, or scream in private. Regret and exasperation need healthy outlets, too. Regain your presence of mind. And then you are better prepared to face another round of dirty tricks. So buy time, however you can manage it.

Get Support

Engaging the mind games that play off of your vulnerabilities is very destabilizing. If you have already lost your footing in dealing with this, it is easy to get caught up in it again. You need to have support. There needs to be a group of trusted individuals who will be there to keep reminding you of what is right, what is true, and what is ultimately best. You need people behind you who believe in you, who uphold your dignity, and who see your potential. It is less important that they understand all the dynamics than they are willing to emotionally support you through the struggle. Do not be afraid to lean on them. There will be a time when you will not to need them as much, but until that time, reach out for their support.

Manipulation wants to control you, subtly. Once you have come to recognize this and believe it, the challenge comes in breaking it. Study the techniques. Learn to identify the patterns. Then begin to engage in the fight. Though you may not be confident of your abilities to fight, it is far more necessary for you to try than to resign. In the trying, you gain clarity, confidence, and direction. But it too is a journey, and not an easy one. You will need courage and strategy. Courage you will have to find within yourself. Strategy is more methodical. Concentrate there first, and it may lend you strength of heart also. Move forward, one step at a time.

The goal through all this? To be able to identify a scam instantly, have the confidence to be unmoved by it, and have the courage to call the bluff. These strategies are meant to build your strength and confidence enough so that you will be able to unmask the manipulation from the outset. When the tricks are clearly revealed as nasty from the start, they not only have no opportunity to do harm, but can also prevent further deception. But this takes time and experience, some failures and lots of practice. As far as you have been restored, stand. The goal is within reach. You must not waver because you have been vulnerable and have fallen before; you must hold your ground. And even more staunchly because you know too well its potential for destruction.

10

PRACTICAL BATTLE STRATEGY

Knowing a strategy and actually applying it are often two different things. Theory is only the mental work; application is the practical work. How to actually go about doing a thing once you have decided that it is the right thing to do is yet another step of courage into the unknown. Having some specific direction is helpful. Below is a list of suggestions. Some may be useful and others not. Use whatever works and gives you strength to keep going on. You are worth it!

Arm yourself with understanding. Knowledge is powerful. Knowing builds confidence, and it assures us of good choices. So start reading. Read about manipulation, control, coercion, power struggles, anger, abuse, co-dependency, narcissism, logical fallacies, powerful dictators, war strategy. Know what it is you are facing. And then *think*!

List the lies. Address your pain rather than dismissing it. Directly face the false implications that he is trying to get you to believe. For example,

I am not worth anyone's trouble.
My efforts are completely inferior.
It is my fault things are in such an upheaval.

Systematically refute them. Know why they are lies. If they are partial truths, deal with the truth and discredit the untruth. When they arise again, refute them again—foremost to yourself.

Play to your strengths. List your strengths, then harness them for your purposes. How can you employ them to: clarify truth, express reality, unveil the tricks, generate income, gain support, earn back some self-respect? For example,

I am good at writing... I can use this to write about my experiences instead of explaining them to others.

Be frank. Likely this has been something you have already tried, but it is too important to omit. Confidently stating your opinions, feelings, and wants is a simple solution that sometimes works. First to yourself, then to he who presses you. It is wise to avoid lengthy explanations, though, because they can easily be dissected to discredit or exploit you. Use simple, absolute statements to respectfully state your stance and nothing more.

"You are mistaken if you think that I agree with you."

Identify the specific strategies your manipulator uses. Note especially what circumstances make you feel awkward, at a disadvantage, or shamed. Make a mental note of the exchange and, later, reflect on what specific strategy he used to get the upper hand. Write it down. Often the dynamics change depending on the audience or lack thereof, so be sure to note that also. And then list possible strategies that you can use to defuse his. Use the encounters that once were designed to manipulate or annihilate you to research your enemy's tactics. There will likely be many, so invest in a fat notebook for this. For example:

Addressing probing and impatient questions
- Request to discuss it later.
- Rephrase questions in light of what is more important.
- Answer slowly and calmly, making eye contact.

Visualize. Rehearse predicted confrontations and review past ones. Analyze where you could have responded better and learn from them. Try to envision yourself doing it, and do what you need to do to give yourself the courage or motivation to follow through the next time.

Find a sympathetic ear. Scoop into your past or into the pool of hesitant onlookers. Often *someone* has noticed things are not quite right. And then they need to listen. It needs to be someone who is going to be in your corner 100 percent. Churches are a good resource, some communities have shelters that can offer some support, and counselors can be. Anyone who believes in you, will make time for you, and is outside of the situation is a good choice.

Post yourself reminders. If you are trying to change your mentality, you will need to pull out all the stops: visual, audio, verbal (even if only from yourself), social. Make seeing clearly your study project. Keep reminding yourself of reality. And let the onlookers think you are crazy. It is better than actually going crazy.

Try to establish concrete measurements. Nail down boundaries. Close the gaps that can be easily exploited. Clear up the grey areas. Be specific but fair. If necessary, be legalistic. Even if there is no cooperation, the refusal to rest on objective standards reveals underlying control. Absolutes threaten manipulation.

Vera and Guy are arguing about allowing their daughter, Rose, to have a pet hamster. Vera is against it, though she will not say why. Guy thinks it will help Rose learn responsibility. There seems to be no way of agreeing, so Guy suggests that they let Rose have a 20 percent input into the decision, with each parent having 40 percent say. To be fair, strong opinions receive full percentage vote while uncertainty reduces the percentage. And Rose must fully understand her commitment.

Keep bringing the issues back to a strictly rational level. Make it clear that the manipulator's aggressive stand is just an opinion. Often manipulation will try to drag the issue into a personal or emotional one. Here his games can be played with much more ease and far less detection. If you instead focus on the rational nature of the decision-making process and the goal of overall good, there is much less room for tricks.

Discard the garbage. Garbage is anything that is designed to create doubt and distract you from uncovering reality. Stay away from it, for it will only draw you into the manipulator's power. Sorting out what is garbage, though, and what is not is very difficult at first. You will make mistakes. You will feel like a heel. You will justify that it probably really was not such a big deal and why did you have to make it into one. But it will get easier. The lines will get clearer. Learning to permit consequences and allow people to be responsible for themselves will come with practice. Do not be discouraged by the rush of guilty emotions. What is important is that you establish boundaries. This will mean drawing firm lines with a confident, "No!" This is a learned skill, so at first, you might misread the situation and throw down some unnecessary ones. That can actually be good, because it unsettles the manipulator, who likely plays off of your reliability. The goal is to be fair, of course, but until you can make those snap judgments, go with your gut. If it feels like a sucker punch, treat it like a sucker punch.

In discarding the garbage, it is also important to pay no attention to that which deserves no attention. Accusations, lies, and distortions are sent to throw you off track, so they are not worth your time. But do not completely ignore them, either. Instead, document them. Sort out their credibility later, if necessary. More importantly, see if you recognize a pattern. When do they arise? What was its real purpose? What made him feel threatened? Then you can better anticipate its reappearance and understand it enough to develop a strategy for countering it.

Disregard the garbage-makers. Stay away from those who will draw you into the manipulator's viewpoint. This is very important, even though it sounds a lot like trying to become narrow-minded. He has probably got you thinking his way by flooding your attention with his perspective already. Give equal time to consider the other side—your side. This will mean cutting off people, so pull away from them graciously. If you will not be supported there, it is time to invest your energies elsewhere, at least until this present crisis has passed. Let them wonder, let them be offended, let them even slander you. They are not worth your tedious explanations anyway. To varying degrees, just walk away.

Beware of these garbage-makers:

- Those who strongly support the manipulator are the obvious garbage-makers. Likely they too are trying to hide behind an illusion. A threat to one established system of control is often a threat to theirs also. It makes their secret fears palatable. So you may also be attacked on that unexpected front. Steer clear of them!

- Those who buy the manipulator's lies are particularly dangerous to you, too. Since they are sincerely believing the illusion, it makes it easier for you to be drawn into it again, too. There was something noble and good about the illusion that drew you into the web in the first place. The temptation is still strongly present. The ideal is still beautiful, except that it is just a sales pitch for something more sinister. Do not let their beliefs sway your convictions. Just stay away.

- It will also mean cutting off people who are trying to find a middle ground. These are the peacemakers who just want to see everyone happy. They believe the answer is in the middle and that if both parties compromise a little, then there can be a peaceful resolution. They are mistaken, for they fail to understand the nature of the beast. Compromise is not a realistic option—not because you are unwilling to give, but because he is (no matter what he claims). Walk away from the offers. This will leave you looking stubborn and uncompromising, but that is exactly what you need to be through this. Later or with normal people: yes! Be open-minded and open-hearted. For now, stand your ground!

Use absolute statements. He clearly has no problem with bold confidence—for himself. It is your turn now. It might feel awkward, but it is an important step to keeping your ground. You know where the lines are that you have been fooled into thinking are largely just grey. Draw them, even if you are not completely certain exactly where. At this point, any line is better than no line. (You can move them later.) Err on the side of high standards. For example, emphatically state:

"I do not answer unfair questions."

Issue a challenge. He may live for a challenge. You are a challenge to him, to see what he can get out of you. Use this. It goes well with frankness and absolute statements: *"This is what I see... Go ahead, prove me wrong."* There might be any sort of pleading, excuses, justifications, or manipulations that follow such a challenge.

Be unmoved. Let the challenge stand. You want to be genuinely convinced. With luck, he will see that you have seen through his tricks, and he may honestly try to rise up to the challenge. Otherwise, keep your distance. The dropped test of character speaks for itself.

Make a scene. As unpleasant as it may be, creating a scene is a good option. You should not act normal if it is unnatural to do! Manipulation plays off of conventions, so it is key to defy convention—calmly, graciously, firmly, and for a purpose. If your manipulator knows you well, he will be able to predict what you will do with fairly good accuracy. You will have to readjust your default reactions at bit to battle this—only temporarily and when there is a threat. But you will need to occasionally apply bold responses, however uncomfortable, to counteract the games.

Accept some corporate sacrifice. Allowing consequences and demanding responsibility will often have some unpleasant side effects on you or others. Let things go awry. Stand back and watch the chaos ensue. Suffer with the loss, let your coworkers suffer with the loss (just make certain they understand why they must), so long as the manipulator is not relieved. It is true that for a time, this suffering might seem worse than just taking on the extra responsibility yourself, but you are achieving something far greater in the process: freedom, respect, and dignity for you all.

Don't try to be a hero, yet. With a skilled manipulator, there is often a number of people who, to various extents, are being fooled or used by him. If they are not yet convinced of the danger they are in, it will take more strength than you can afford to convince them otherwise. If they do know and are also suffering under the tyranny, they are a good source of support. They too will be struggling and not have a good idea of what to do about it, either. If this is so, it is even more important that you rise up against the control. But you will have to leave them behind to some extent. Worry about rescuing them later. You need to focus on securing your own strength. Fight your way out first, and then turn to humanitarian service.

Unveil the true motivation. By far, the most effective method is exposing the underlying motivations publicly, but this is extremely difficult to orchestrate. The idea is not simply to expose his shame—for then you would be no better than he is—but to press him into choosing between his noble-looking facade and his true motivations. The unchecked selfishness will show itself. This is what you want people to see clearly anyway, not all the specific incidents.

Seek some formal judgment of justice. This may involve the legal system (though risky and costly, it is an option of last resort) or not. If there is some other source of objectivity and authority that both parties will respect, or at least must abide by, that ought to be considered. Whomever is chosen however must not be personally involved in the situation, must have a strong sense of integrity himself, and must not be easily swayed by emotional appeal. The judge must be immune to the tricks and must have genuine authority to enact consequences. If he does not, then he is just another pawn in the game of deceit, and you are better off without him.

eGo now, and fight the good fight.

11
LETTING GO

YOU HAVE BEEN DRAWN IN to invest your absolute best with bright hopes that turned out to be elusive, been cruelty exploited despite your best efforts to keep the peace, been forced to battle gross injustice with few resources and very little support, and just managed to claw your way out with countless gaping, emotional wounds. Struggling to make your cause clear has proven to be difficult with the inexhaustible deceit, so even the authorities have withheld complete justice. So you are left with a muddle of mixed results. Even without the garbage still coming, there is still the aftermath. The mess to clean up looks overwhelming. In struggling to survive and battle, much of the lesser concerns were neglected—and rightly so. But those are the issues that need your attention now: the lingering loss, the pain, the confusion, the weariness. Those must be sorted also. Is there no end to this trial? *Absolutely yes!*

Though you may not yet realize it, you have been made strong through the struggle. You have developed keen understanding and valuable skills that are a rich resource to the people around you. You have a far greater depth than at first. And you have demonstrated great courage. You have taken a firm stand for truth and justice. The fight itself has been a powerful testimony to the universal importance of your cause. Reality needed to be revealed. Dignity needs courageous advocates. Freedom was worth it. You are worth it.

With the bulk of the tension relieved, you can turn your attention to trying to make some sense of it all. Some of the nagging "whys" of the chaos can be answered. It offers some closure when the results are still unsatisfying, and it is a safeguard for you. It helps to see more clearly to know best what to keep and what to leave behind. Moving forward is hard enough without having to sort through all the baggage blindly. So take some time to try to understand it a bit, and then let the unhelpful parts go.

Goodbye to the Manipulation Dance

The more you try to anchor yourself with truth and reason, the fiercer the storm becomes. Frantically trying to bail out your water-logged boat, you cease looking to anchor. Eventually, though, the storm does stop, but you are worn out and raw from the trial. In time, you might recover enough to begin your search again, but then another storm suddenly hits. All your energy is absorbed in preventing a disaster, again. Eventually, you notice a pattern and the only way to keep from being drowned is to keep the peace. Float along with wherever the elements lead you and you will have no reason to fear. Keep the master of the storms happy and you will stay afloat. So goes the dance.

While manipulation from the perspective of the manipulated is inexplicable and staggeringly difficult to manage, there is reason (though not good reason) behind the madness. Manipulators are suffering from a great deal of pain, even if they will not admit it. Somehow their efforts to self-soothe, ease the pain, and address problems directly have failed. Long or intense experience must have convinced them that these approaches are futile. So deeply disappointed, they have rejected justice and natural order and set up a new standard and means of control: manipulation. They conclude that since society has rejected caring for them naturally, they will have to fool them into doing it. Their purpose is to get other people to solve their problems for them or at least to take the blame for the failures. It is their means of survival, driven by their insecurity. They are seeking stability, and they find that others do offer that. Others *can* protect and provide. They can act as buffers against the blows of life, and they can help meet the needs and wants of those around them. Though it comes at the cost of their self-sacrifice, it can be done. And it does provide some sense of security.

To him, a relationship is "every man for himself"—but by sugar-coating it with charm and finesse, he finds he does have an advantage. He is driven to take what he wants while making it appear perfectly innocent. To him, the end justifies the means, and there is little motivation to adopt a different policy. He is master. While this may give him a rush of power, it is secretly destroying the social foundation. Without objective standards and common expectations, insecurity reigns—even for the chaos-maker.

Most chronic relational problems are cycles. Fear, anxiety, or misunderstanding feed behaviors that trigger negative reactions in the other person. This then leads to more fear, anxiety, misunderstanding, or whatever else, while doing little to offer relief to either party. If left unchecked, this can continue for years until the relationship completely degrades. Clearly steps should to be taken to stop a doomed downward spiral.

With manipulation, his insecurity grasps for control, his control undermines relationships, and bruised relationships heighten insecurity. Beyond surface appearances, everyone is miserable and scrambling. And it is entirely possible that no one caught in the cycle recognizes this. The manipulator is too absorbed with his schemes to notice, and those under his thumb are often too desperate struggling to find answers and relief. The cycle clearly must be broken.

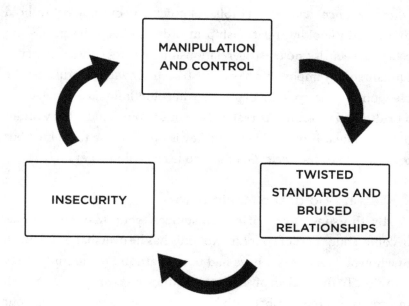

With a cycle of control, though the illusions may suggest you are largely to blame, your contribution as the victim is far from obvious. You can never be a source of perfect security for anyone. You have no influence over the past. The deep insecurity was likely there long before you entered the picture. Nor, as you probably have discovered, do you have much influence over his determination to use control. It appears that the only way to break the cycle as the victim is to prevent the control from doing damage.

If the control does not harm your relationship, then manipulation can work. If you are not bothered by the games, then you *can* stop contributing to the cycle: you can ignore them or resign yourself to being controlled. Ignoring it can be effective temporarily, but the stakes will likely continue to rise until you cannot ignore it any longer. Resigning yourself to being controlled, while possible, undermines your purpose, identity, and dignity. It is feasible, but it is hardly healthy. Control will have its impact. Manipulation, despite your resilience, will take its toll. As much as you may try to hold to a healthy-looking relationship in order to keep the peace and establish security, no trusting relationship involves control. And it is fundamentally impossible to establish security without trust. So the one point of the cycle that appears you could influence (preventing a bruised relationship) is really also out of your hands. No wonder life feels like it is utter chaos. The key is not to cease to be hurt but to break out of the cycle. Get out and leave it alone. Let it go.

Letting Go of the Manipulator

By the sheer force of circumstances, your manipulator has become a huge part of your life. Not only has he overshadowed much of who you are, but you have had to turn around to carefully study him also. To the neglect of almost everything else, you found yourself in a multi-layered combat with him. It required great focus on your part, so your understanding of him has only deepened. This level of focus is comparable to the concentration it took in trying to keep the manipulative tricks in check before the fight. So it turns out that he has absorbed most of your attention through the oppression and through the battle. You have invested *so* much into this man!

So your manipulator may be all you have really known for years. Now you know him better. And he is familiar. It may be a very appealing idea to try to redeem the losses rather than cutting them. Maybe you can even salvage a happy ending out of all this mess. After all, somewhere beneath all the deception and tricks is a vulnerable man with an incredible understanding of human nature. There is great potential in him for good. It might seem generous to offer terms of peace and restoration. Indeed, it would be easier for you, for it would save you having to completely restructure your life. But do not act in haste! While possibly subdued, the manipulation is still lurking and waiting its chance to rise again. It is what he knows and what is familiar and comfortable to him, so that is where he wants to return.

Though the potential for what he could become is likely great, what he has become overshadows it. The behavior hinders the possibilities. Your presence, by no fault of your own, has contributed to his irresponsibility. He knows you far too well and cares about you far too little for you to be safe with him. Letting down your guard and making yourself available to him is only an invitation for him to invade again. Without a definitive change of his heart, you can do nothing for him. As much as he needs help and support to overcome his own insecurities, you cannot open his eyes to this truth. You cannot make him see that there is a better way to live. Your presence will not motivate him to change. You cannot, so let him go.

Letting Others Go

To an almost unbelievable extent, others play a huge role in the manipulation game. Emerging from the heat of the battle, you are vulnerable. Your keen alertness to one source of danger makes you more susceptible to unexpected dangers from other directions. Other people are still going to be there and will still be pushing your pressure points, even unknowingly. They have set ideas and will be promoting them to your still shaky confidence. You likely care about them, but many of them will only end in doing you harm. Throw up all the boundaries that you need to against them, because first and foremost, you need to be safe to heal.

There was probably a great number of people you had to let go in the battle, those who were well-meaning but only hindered the purpose. There is nearly always a crowd of interested people anxious to help with shallow maxims and blind advice. They are sincere and caring, but they do not understand. These people are still a source of undeserved doubt and guilt to you. As much as you may want to restore your relationships with them, they will still not be helpful through your healing. They are ghosts of the past, and while you should deal with them politely, they do not belong in your intimate circle. They have proven to be untrustworthy—not by their own character flaw but because they are trusting, even partially, in an illusion. They still do not believe, and it is still not worth it to try to make them see. Leave them be.

There are others who, through your battle, have likely become adamantly opposed to you. You have drawn a line and have stood resolutely for your beliefs, and that always drives strong divisions. People have rallied around him in support of his cause, which means that they are against you. So by fighting your way to freedom, you have likely made more enemies than just your manipulator. On top of everything else, this may be difficult to bear. But the people that you have driven away by speaking up for truth and standing firmly for justice are not the people that you want to know. Likely, they too are threatened by these things—be they manipulators themselves or not—so they will gladly despise you. Pay them no heed. Rather bear their scorn as a badge of honor because that is a sure sign that you *are* doing something great.

And then there are the new victims. Undoubtedly with your withdrawal, there will be others recruited to fill the void your absence has created. They may be people whom you know and like or new innocents recruited from afar. Wherever they come from, they are likely big-hearted people who have not been trained to recognize deceit, either. So quite ignorantly, they too are drawn deeper and deeper into the control, going perhaps even cheerfully and willingly—at first. But you know what is really happening despite what it appears, and you know where it leads. It is dreadful to watch. Yet explaining it all makes you look crazy to the disbelieving. The manipulator has absolutely already discredited you, so speaking up would only reaffirm his distorted claims. Leave your actions to speak for themselves. They too need to follow their own journeys of discovering the deeply sinister undertow. Let your life and your increasing freedom be your testimony. There is no rescuing he who does not believe he needs to be rescued. Making yourself available to these people will likely only make you relive your own pain while doing no real good for anyone at all. They can come to you when they decide you were right. Until then, let them go.

Letting go of people is especially difficult because it feels like ceasing to care. It is pulling them out of your heart so that they no longer impact you emotionally, and that means there is loss. It is a goodbye and it can be bitter. But you must believe it is for a greater sweetness. Once you are strong again, then they can become a greater part of your life, but in a healthier balance. For now, though, they need to be kept well away from your affections. Their influence will not be for good.

Old Purposes Must Pass

With freedom, you may find a void in your identity and purpose. Being a victim gave you an identity, even if it was not a healthy one. It gave you a purpose: to strive against the odds for scraps of dignity. Then the battle gave you a new identity: defender of justice. Your purpose was noble, good, and right. Your fight was just, and you were striving with all your might for ideals greater than yourself. There was vision and purpose. However slow the progress, it did prove to be successful to some extent. But now that chapter is closed, too. If you have just come fresh out into freedom, things may look phenomenally fuzzy. All your focus has been directed towards relief, and now that you have some, it can be disorienting knowing what to do next.

Just as you had to let go of the victim mentality, so you must let go of the battle mentality. While you still need to be on your guard against manipulative tricks, that should not be your main concentration anymore. It was only a battle, not a lifestyle. Those skills that you developed will still be there when the need arises. Until then, they need to be packed away. You need to make room for brighter things. This can feel like loss also, though, because you have spent so much time, pain, and energy developing these abilities, and now it appears they are just to be set aside. It is yet another risk, after such a long series of losses already, to let the battle go, too. It might take time to learn to put down the heightened vigilance and keen suspicions, to refrain from boldly peeling away layers of motivation and emphatically laying down boundary lines. As it took time to take them up, it will take time to lay them down. There is no urgency now, though, but there should be a steady loosening of your grip. Before you can move onto healing, you must make room for peace and joy.

Forgiveness

With more freedom, your thoughts are also freer. Instead of focusing on survival strategies, battle tactics, and countermeasures, you can pause long enough to step back and look at the mess. Rather than scrambling to prevent disaster, you can see more objectively that it was all a complete abomination. Likely, the farther you get from the oppression, the more you will notice how cruel the attacks actually were, how absurdly unnecessary the control is, and how needlessly he has made you suffer—much more so than you might have first suspected. Indeed, he may still be making you suffer. The physiological atrocities he commits are insufferable. He ought to be stopped; his behavior should be intolerable; he needs to pay. Even though you likely know his depravity better than anyone else, it is not yours to repay the wrongs. Cut the ties, set him adrift with all the bitterness he has caused you, and sail into the sunset without it: forgive.

Forgiveness: not foolish trust or unmerited favor or excuses. Not a concession of the fight or an unfounded loosening of vigilance. But it refuses to extend the fight from one for justice to one of revenge. It has an underlying sorrow that your opponent is caught so deeply in deceit that he cannot see the better way, so you must fight. Not because he personally is evil but because what he is choosing to do is.

Forgiveness is a promise not to retaliate. It releases the bitterness and rage inside of you and refuses to entertain them any longer. Though you have been disgracefully treated and unjustly used, though the blows you have borne from him and for him are likely innumerable, though he has managed to wreak havoc of nearly everything most dear and fundamental to you, you cannot make him pay for his crimes. It does not mean that you cannot appeal to an authority for justice nor that you hinder natural consequences nor that you set yourself up to be violated again. It does not mean that you should trust him or help him or honor him. Forgiveness is no promise of restoration. It is not foolish trust, broad-minded excuses, or denial. It does not justify evil. But it does let go.

He has hurt you deeply and thoroughly. Your trust has been completely broken. You cannot forget what he has done, and you must protect yourself against what he will continue to do. He will have consequences to bear because of his behavior, which you should not prevent. But forgiveness promises not to hurt him as he has hurt you. It will not stoop to becoming like him by making him suffer because you have suffered. It lets go of the responsibility to personally enact justice. Neither, though, should you interfere with the natural consequences—be it through an authority or based on normal relational dynamics. His guilt still rests squarely on his own shoulders, and you need to leave it there. Forgiveness steps back to make room for other people or principles to deal with that guilt. Your role is done in making it known. By forgiving, you hope that justice will be served so that lessons will be learned. You will be happy to see the day that he is sorry enough to change.

With the end of the war, your purpose has changed—and so have your needs. What is not of value any longer, as precious as it had become, ought to be left behind. That which has ceased to help you make progress, regardless of the mess it is still in, needs to be set adrift. Before you can move forward to embrace all the richness that liberty offers, you need to let go of the manipulator and his dance, the misguided opinions of others, your old identities, and all the hatred manipulation has stirred up inside of you. They will only hold you back. Make room for something better. Loosen your grip on them so that you can be truly free.

12
MOVING FORWARD

Once you have come to let go of that which you could from the past, it is time to turn your attention elsewhere. The present still has its struggles: you must continue to deal with any manipulation that raises its ugly head, you must keep contending with your lingering doubts and fears, and you still must battle the misguided opinions of others. But, for once, your focus should not be there. It is time to turn your attention to the future. You need to move on. It is time to regain your footing and direction. Manipulation has prevented you from moving forward for far too long. Freedom gives you the ability to shed all the obligations and bondage, to let them go and leave them behind. This is a whole new chapter, the beginning of a new story. It is time to use all your great talents and skills for something worthwhile now!

Rebuilding and restoration are good first steps. Pursue wholeness, and then pursue fullness of life. So initially, you need to address the practical needs: how will you replace the things you lost? A house, a car, a job, your connections. What you have not replaced already needs some of your attention. You need a vision and a plan. But so does your own well-being. You need a vision and a plan for healing. Find out what it is going to take to live again. And if you were unable to make a complete break with your manipulator, it is important to know what his genuine healing would look like, too.Maintain stout boundaries for as long as there remains a threat but heal within the safety of your walls.

The Manipulator's Road to Healing

Chronic manipulation is a way of life, a pattern of thinking, and a finely honed skill. Even though it is dreadfully harmful and does not really work, letting it go is terrifying. It means putting down the only guard he has against the shame, vulnerability, and insecurities locked deep within his heart. It means risking nearly every method he has for handling the pains of life. Beyond requiring admitting he has been choosing badly, he has to trust the very people he has scorned and used before. Understandably, the step is a big one—one that he is unlikely to take without motivation and support. Exposing that insecurity was unthinkable enough to resort to manipulation in the first place.

But the answer to insecurity is reassurance. Those who are uncertain need stability. They need to know objective standards and justice, affirmation for genuine good, and that they have someone strong and concerned enough to lean on through the process. Very much like helping a toddler learn to walk or raising a child through the "terrible twos," he needs someone present to catch him in his falls and sometimes endure a temper tantrum. With the terrifying step of allowing deep-rooted shame to be exposed for the first time possibly in decades, there needs to be a great deal of affirmation and support. He needs to know that he is accepted while his behavior is not.

Hurting people do hurt people. What they need is a tough love. Ironically, those who deserve it the least need to be loved the most. But it must be a love that is without fear, that sees clearly and entertains no nonsense. A love that will draw the hard lines. A love that understands there is hurt deeply buried and is not afraid to dig it up. A love that works for his best despite himself, one that will stop giving him what he wants and start giving him what he needs. A love that will not only dodge the blows without wavering but will apply them as justice demands. A mighty tough love. A confident love. Yet one filled with great hope. His supporters must turn away from tender openness and begin promoting restoration based on truth. They must nurture only within the boundaries of justice and reality, not beyond them. There is some agony that should not taste sympathy because it is guiding a soul to a freeing truth. Let him agonize, for that is what he needs most.

The key to curing manipulation is not much different from the key to curbing it. Insecurity grasps control because it feels like there is no control otherwise. By establishing firm boundaries, an intolerance for tricks, and a foundation based on a more objective reality, you are building security. There is someone who is in some control—not to control others but to hold to a standard. A standard that is clear and dependable, concrete enough to lean on, strong enough to resist opposition. This is stability—something that can be counted on to withstand the blows of life. Even if you are not directing the healing, your firm stand is probably doing just as much good for him as it is for you.

His road to healing will be difficult, and you have no control over whether he will take that step or not. There are no guarantees. There is no sure cure to willful blindness and stout denial of reality. A physician can only do so much to promote health—the patient must also be willing to be healed and put in his effort, too. You can hold out hope for a recovery, but you cannot count on a miracle. Your greater hope is in investing into what you know is good—a good that reveals itself in obvious, practical ways. Reclaim yourself. Rise to your own protection and those you love. Move onto better things. Perhaps someday that may include turning to help your oppressor or leaving him alone to his fate. Whichever path you must take, know that you have done your best. And that is all you can ever do.

Healing the Relationship

Healing the relationship is impossible if manipulation is still happening. Period. For ongoing cruelty, there needs to be complete independence before there can be any healing. An established manipulative system cannot be fought from within. There is little you can do when there is still no respect or willingness to compromise. Trust is unable to grow under the shadow of control. You must come out of it first. You must have the ability to ignore the control without severe repercussions. You must have the clarity and confidence to hold to a hard standard. And if nothing works, you must be able walk away without guilt or consequence. Then you are in a better position to take authority—not to overshadow but to guide.

While not impossible, the cure is by no means easy. And in all likelihood, he will not go there as long as you are available to feed his appetites. So your freedom is vital for his healing as well. Yet still, his healing is possible only after he has been through most of his own journey out of bad choices. He needs to be committed to change. But with so many levels of deceit, this is difficult to judge. You will have to decide if the relationship is worth salvaging based on his genuine efforts to make things right.

When there is a rift in a relationship, there naturally is a distancing. The bigger the rift, the greater the distance. This is both necessary and healthy. In general, this should not to be simply accepted or ignored; there ought to be some response to make things better. When the rift has a definite cause—in our case, ongoing manipulation—the path back to a functional relationship is two-fold: forgiveness and repentance.

Your part, as a victim, is to forgive. Forgiveness is a letting go. First, justice is left in the hands of the ruling authority, even if that is only natural consequences. Then it takes the offense that has occurred and incorporates it into a new reality—one that is clearly less ideal than would have been. It eventually accepts the situation, as regrettable as it may be, and leaves the offender to struggle with himself without interference from you. It is not a dismissal, but a reluctant embrace. It does not mean that we should like the situation, trust the manipulator, or break our necks and hearts to please him any longer. But it does mean that we are free to move on, allowing healing for ourselves and opening the possibility of restoring the relationship under the right conditions.

Forgiveness, if accompanied with repentance, is restoring and purifying. It takes us off the path of strained vigilance to one of mutual benefit, alliance, and peace. Without denying the past, it renews life and steps boldly into the hope of a new future. It gives a vote of confidence and a fresh start to the offender. It is the hoped-for happy ending to all broken relationships. And it is beautiful, but it *requires* the offender to change. There must be a permanent ceasefire before peace can exist.

The offender has a vital responsibility, which should never be taken lightly. If people insist that your forgiveness is key to restoring the relationship, they are only half right. The offender must repent too. He must agree in mind, heart, word, and action that what he has done was cruel and hurtful. He must be willing to own his guilt and do everything he can to make it right again. If he does not, you have no grounds for trusting him. You cannot believe a deceiver while he is continuing to deceive.

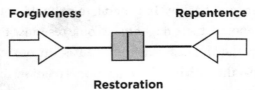

Forgiveness   **Repentence**

Restoration

With weariness, self-doubt, outside pressures, and illusions, it may be tempting to settle for something less. So much depends on the offender changing, it might seem there can be peace some other way. Often it appears that if we can stretch ourselves a little further than just forgiving, we can meet him a little more on his terms and things will be better. It may be justified as offering him mercy, but really it only excuses him from his responsibilities and hinders true healing. The indulgence may come in the form of ignoring, trusting without merit, or excuses, but it always fails to restore. True forgiveness neither removes consequences, even emotional ones, nor promotes injustice. It requires the offender to serve his full sentence to prove he has learned and that he is willing to stretch himself all the way to restoration. He needs to do his part 100 percent.

Imitations of forgiveness try to go beyond its duty to alleviating some of the manipulator's uncomfortable guilt. They lower the standard of behavior to make it somehow more achievable for the offender, which also diminishes the severity of his offense. But in trying to remove the sting of guilt, you trivialize your own suffering and make true repentance unnecessary.

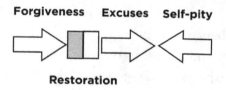

While this will likely ease the suffering of the offender, it ultimately does him no favors. Short-lived warmth of feeling soon gives way to repeated offenses. Guilty actions must have guilty punishments. The degree of the consequences should be dictated by justice, not by sympathy.

Mercy does give some flexibility to the exact essence of a reconciliation; the standard does have some ability to move. It does extend a hand to help him whom *cannot* restore himself. But mercy should not be lightly given when there has proven to be consistent deception. It should be reserved for the *real* inability (physical limitations or the logical impossibilities of making complete amends). It should never be offered for moral or character weakness, elaborate rhetoric, weak or dramatic efforts, or claimed ignorance. There must be enough evidence that he has stopped attacking and has truly changed for you to have grounds to begin to trust him. The efforts must be absolutely genuine. Anything less will result in an easy relapse into old habits, at your expense *again*. This indeed is a tall order but absolutely necessary. On your part: forgiveness must always come; mercy has no such obligation.

Stretching out forgiveness shows a willing spirit, but it is a dangerous practice. Trying to restore a relationship while there is still a strong hand of control is self-destructive. Complete repentance is absolutely necessary for healing a manipulative relationship. As uncomfortable as facing guilt may be, it is crucial. It must penetrate every aspect of the man before he can be restored and begin to earn your trust back. Intellectually, he must understand his actions and their effects as being devastating. Facing this reality must hurt dreadfully—it must powerfully touch his emotions. And encountering all this truth must be potent enough to sink into his behavior. There must be change: change in motivation, perspective, and action. True repentance shows. And it must be obvious even to you: he needs to initiate a sincere expression of regret to all the offended parties, he must be willing to accept the full consequences for his actions without weaseling, and he should make all possible amends with a generous spirit. And then this change must stand the test of time.

The Earmarks of Repentance
1. Realization
2. Remorse
3. Repentance
4. Recompense
5. Reliability

No rushing and no shortcuts are acceptable.

If the signs are not all there, absolutely forgive but do not trust. Forgiveness has reached it limit. You have done all that you can do along these lines. Focus your attention somewhere else worthwhile.

Healing for Yourself

Enduring abuse is a sign of great strength. Fighting for your own self-respect, moral standards, and identity in the face of relentless cruelty requires a rare fortitude. It can take everything inside of you just to keep surviving. It requires perseverance despite your complete vulnerability, your eroded dignity, the merciless treatment, and no vision. You pull yourself back up from being trampled once again, knowing all too well that it is just a matter of time before you will be shoved back down. You are strong to bear the blows and stronger by refusing to retaliate, despite the gross injustice. After each defeat—beaten, discouraged, and left barely alive—you still rise again. Despite the ceaseless attacks and cruel blows, you have not been destroyed. And *that* is incredible strength.

But fighting to get out of abuse requires a different kind of strength: one that sets aside the defensive strategies to apply offensive ones. Having the courage to shed the victim mentality and step out into the heat of the battle, without experience or guarantee, is impressive. There is no easing into the onslaught since you are already deep in it, and you must face not only a formidable opponent but also doubt and the despair of failure. It is beyond just being convinced that it is worthwhile. It is risking every precious scrap of yourself that you have left for something better. And that is *huge*! But it is also a process, a process which involves a large investment—of time, energy, resources, and trust. It requires you to gain completely new skills and apply them with great confidence. It means that you keep fighting even when it seems you are losing. It means picking yourself up, all bruised and aching, to get back out there to keep fighting this evil. You are there, not at all because you want to be, but because you are hope. There is a better tomorrow, and it depends on you.

The shift from normality into a victim mentality was one from health to helplessness to hopelessness. Digging your way out means undoing the thought patterns that got you down so low. Rising up to fight manipulation is your first step, lifting you from hopelessness by enacting justice. You develop the strategies and strength to fight and to fight well. And in the process, you send the message that you are no longer willing to tolerate the games; you have renounced acceptance of the mistreatment. And that is where you need to stay as long as the battle is intense enough to demand your full attention. But once the dust has settled, there is still another step to the healing: securing you freedom.

If the manipulation was severe and the fight out of it intense, the journey to health, happiness, and stability is not over. Even if you have been able to completely break the bonds with your manipulator and his behavior (which is uncommon), the aftermath is still a mess. Thought patterns from the victim mentality likely still linger, and defense mechanisms from the fight may be easily stirred. Plus, you are coming out of a battle raw with deep emotional wounds. These, with time and attention, can be tempered. They *can* fall into the background of a more balanced life, but it is still going to take some work.

Enduring under manipulation for any length of time changes your thinking. You have been conditioned by the merciless tricks to expect to be taken advantage of. That is how you could survive, and that thought pattern is likely still present. If you still have lingering expectations that you will be used, you are still vulnerable to being used. It does not just automatically go away. It is going to take effort and risk again to develop new skills. Thankfully, this time, not within a hostile environment.

With the threat subdued, circumstances have changed. You can embrace new expectations now. Expect to be treated with respect. Expect your voice to be heard, your feelings to be considered, your dreams to matter, your ideas to have some influence. Expect that people will be fair and reasonable. Expect that justice is a high ideal that ought to be upheld by all. Trust your judgment, your feelings, your experiences, your abilities. Believe in your potential. And most importantly, be prepared to protect your dignity.

As much as you know anticipating blows is no longer needed, either, it takes some time to let it sink into your heart, too. Be patient with yourself, even if others are not. Surround yourself with compassionate people who will let you heal at your own pace. Living in freedom without threat does take some adjustment, but it is good. Build new friendships with trustworthy people. Find ways to serve others. Begin to build into that which will have good results. You could use a little success, so go in that direction. Remember who you used to be and who you used to want to be. Now is the time to embrace all that is good about yourself.

Because you have engaged the battle, you now possess a new power and respect that you may not realize. It is the ability to erect boundaries and enact consequences. You might be haunted by memories of it failing before, so you may not want to try. You also know all too well how it can be misused, so it is tempting to avoid it altogether. But because you have been through the fire, you are in a far better position than nearly anyone else to know how important power is and how to use it with care. All the agony has given you clarity, wisdom, conviction, and confidence. Though you may not know it yet, you now are able to balance justice and mercy, truth and compassion, boundaries and kindness, shrewdness and acceptance in perfect harmony. Both skill sets are within you, and you have used them both enough to know their weaknesses and strengths. Now use them wisely and well.

And lastly, alas, there is still one more hurdle: sorting through all the baggage left from the chaos. Likely a tremendous amount of shame, doubt, anger, regret, failure, and pain has built up. You have suffered great loss and shattered dreams, so there is grief and sorrow, too. Your heart is heavily burdened. In the heat of the battle, these troubles were neglected. But once you are out, they do need to be methodically faced. You need to rant about the cruelty, mourn over the loss, and cry over the hurt. You may need to revisit some of the pain you refused to feel before. You need to dig up some of the memories that have been pressed down. You need to let yourself feel all of those things that you could not process before: ugly, uncomfortable, painful things. Carrying such a heavy weight will not benefit anyone. As weary as you may be of struggling and how much you may want to just forget the pain, it has still become a part of you. Before you can move on, it needs to be faced and sorted and, only then, left behind. In time and when you are ready, and then maybe just bit by bit...

The shift of strengths under manipulation is strenuous, so the news of more strain might be very unwelcome. If it is too overwhelming, give yourself time. You need to feel safe first. Rest in the presence of those who have supported you through this. Make your haven a place of beauty and peace. Begin investing into your dreams again. Find some happiness. And when you are ready, reach out for the "something more," for there is even deeper joy ahead.

Levels of Strength

Strength to Endure	Strength to Fight	Strength of Freedom
Endurance to tolerate the problem	Determination to battle with the problem	Assurance to rise above the problem
Goal of survival	Vision for justice	Vision for balance
Defensive	Offensive	Responsive
Passively engaged with manipulation	Actively engaged against manipulation	Disengaged from manipulation

The transfer of strengths is important. You need to adjust to the changes in circumstances. But you are strong, and there is an end to the journey. And at the end is not only freedom from oppression but also freedom of spirit. Strangely, shame and insecurities lose a great deal of their power once you have passed through the fire. Reality seems so much clearer, and your confidence in it becomes natural. Much fear is dissolved, and hope does not seem so impossibly far away. Love can flow freely, and people notice a compelling difference in you. Life still has all of its troubles and woes, but they are not so overwhelming if you have already lived through hell. And once you reach a strength of freedom, the intense struggle within is also over. Life has begun: richer, fuller, and freer.

Welcome to joy, at last!

EPILOGUE

THIS JOURNEY IS MY JOURNEY. For nearly two decades, I lived in isolation, fear, helplessness, and hopelessness. There was no one, *no one* who really saw, believed, or understood. Struggling to gain some sort of footing and protect my children, to hold onto any shred of dignity and find some answers, I slowly sank into utter despair. Fighting against the odds, day in and day out, completely alone and without vision, life was nothing but a shell. The harder I tried to make things better, the worse they got. The only person whom I could turn to for strength was the one who was determined to suck the very life out of me. And I had little choice but to let him.

But perhaps my story would help...

Engineer, mother, teacher, writer, and victim...but no longer. My life started out as a success story with good potential and then took a twenty-year detour into a nightmare. Shortly after college, I married an energetic and dynamic man with lofty ambitions and a curious magnetism that seemed to get people to anxiously contribute to whatever scheme he had going on. Ever so slowly, I began to realize what this superhuman power over people was, and it was not good. By that time, however, knee-deep in small children and isolated from any sort of significant personal support, I was solidly stuck. I tried every non-violent theory: turning the other cheek, killing with kindness, reasonable explanations, submission, contentment, pity, direct confrontation, passive resistance, expressing my feelings, suppressing my feelings, offering creative compromises, and finally years of dogged perseverance. They were all artfully undermined or completely un-beneficial. Overburdened, tired, alone, confused, and with nothing left to enter into any sort of battle, I sank into the victim mentality. Tunnel-vision (refusing to look at anything except the immediacy) was the only thing that worked. Life was a prison. But I *had* to survive, if only for the sake of my children.

By the time my sixth child was due, I knew my strength would be completely spent. At that point, I was homeschooling four, caring for a toddler, running a house, gardening, canning, milking, taking care of poultry, doing home repairs, cleaning (barely), and trying to stave off complete despair—all with very meager resources. The laundry alone kept me tied to the house. And though I had so little energy, regularly I would use it to throw myself between the children and harm's way—the unreasonable demands, the harsh criticisms, the impossible expectations, the thankless work, and the shifting standards. Times were desperate, while he was floating on air. So I began my research...

Unmasking Manipulation emerged through trying to make sense of it all. As my husband came from a family with other toxic people (also manipulating us), I had plenty of ongoing experience with both the techniques and repercussions of manipulation. In coming to the realization that this was not just my lot to bear but my obstacle to overcome, I made a thorough and systematic study of the manipulative tricks around me and approaches for defusing their subtle lies. Then, with a confused mix of fear and faith, I applied them. While many of my efforts have been satisfying, the journey has been long and bitter and indeed will likely never be completely over. But I have grown much in my convictions: that deceit is evil, that human dignity is worth fighting viciously for, that mind games can only be matched by shrewdness, and that developing strength is a tiresome but vital journey. Alas, though, there has been no clear, happy ending. The manipulation is still pouring out; he has not changed. So it is a daily battle to stand for justice, to uncover the truth, to remain vigilant, to untangle the tricks, and to dispel the lies. Every day is a battle in the mind, in the heart, in the spirit—not to sink. Yet every day, we are a little stronger, a little more convinced of the power of truth, and a little bit nearer to happiness. At last, we have hope.

"With man this is impossible, but with God all things are possible."
Matthew 19:26

Though the details of my story are not so important, I want you to know: I have been there. I know the helplessness. I know the wishing that the blows were physical so you could just prove the abuse. I know the pain does not ever really go away. I know the sting of well-meaning people betraying you because they do not fully believe. I know the haunting doubts that you did not try hard enough. I know how easy it is to believe the lies that people will throw at you completely unexpectedly. I know the regret of having made the choice to let him into your life at all. I know the overwhelming temptation to just throw it all away and attack him on the same level he is attacking you. I know. And my journey is not nearly over, either, so I share your pain.

APPENDIX

Logical Fallacies

Logical fallacies are a form of distorting the truth that are freely applied by manipulators. They introduce untruth by following unsound reasoning. Somewhere there is a subtle error between what is actually given and what is concluded. If you can identify this, discrediting the trick is easy. This skill is clearly to your advantage when trying to untangle illusions. The drawback is that they focus on logical reasoning, which is difficult to unpack in the heat of the moment. Though limited in application, they do offer an objective standard. If you can become familiar with them enough to identify them, even after the fact, you will see how you are being duped. You are not the crazy one after all! This is a whole branch of study, but for practical unmasking, it is helpful to be familiar with the common ones. You may notice a strong similarity to some of the tactics already discussed.

Three Main Categories of Logical Fallacies
- **Fallacies of relevance:** These distract you from the argument to some side issue that is not relevant to the conclusion. Often it will attack the person or appeal to some illegitimate standard rather than trying to find the truth from the facts. These include ridicule, threats, and emotional appeal.

- **Fallacies of ambiguity:** These use unclear meanings or connections to muddy the real issue. They use confusion to direct the argument to his desired conclusion rather than following sound reasoning. These include word games and presenting theory as fact.
- **Fallacies of presumption:** These assume something from the beginning that is not completely right—what is claimed to be true is not, so what is concluded from it is invalid. These include loaded questions, hasty generalizations, and false dilemmas.

Fallacies of Relevance

Red Herring: This relies on redirecting the focus to an irrelevant piece of information that might appear to support his point. This would include holding a double standard or introducing unreasonable exceptions to a rule.

"Work harder to get this done for me today! You need to because it isn't in my job description."

Ipse dixit: This is an illegitimate appeal to authority. It implies that because one person (possibly the arguer) believes a statement, regardless of his lack of expertise, that you should also.

"Even the neighbors can see that the car you bought is a lemon."

Ad populum: This is an illegitimate appeal to popularity. It suggests that because it is a popular belief, it must be a true belief.

"You'd like a beard. It's the latest style."

Ad baculum: This is an illegitimate appeal to force. It presses its point with threats (genuine or empty).

"If you don't, you'll be sorry. I'll see to that."

Ad hominem: This is a verbal attack on the person rather than his argument.

"You have absolutely no sense."

Bulverism: This attacks a position by pointing out how the arguer came to hold it.

"You only think that because that is what your mother says."

Tu quoque: This attacks the arguer by pointing out an inconsistency between his actions and his argument.

"You're one to say it is important to exercise! You're not in shape, either."

Fallacy of pleasantness: This suggests that because a claim is not pleasant, it is therefore not true.

"Was that a nice thing to say? I'll listen when you find something nice to say."

Appeal to the stone: This simply dismisses an assertion as absurd without further proof.

"That is just silly. It's not even worth my attention."

Broken window fallacy: This points to a localized benefit generated from the situation, while ignoring the larger losses, to justify the action as good.

"You could use a new window anyway. That one was drafty. So I did you a favor by breaking it."

Slippery slope: This claims that a few small first steps will lead to an inevitably bad conclusion, so they should not be taken.

"If you decide to leave, everyone will follow you, and all we have invested in will fail."

Ad ignorantiam: This assumes a statement is true because no one has proven it false.

"My bad language doesn't bother anyone. Nobody ever complains."

Chronological snobbery: This is an argument based merely on the passage of time, either its longevity supports its truth or its novelty supports that it is an improvement.

"This new upgrade will be great!"

Fallacies of Ambiguity

Equivocation: This changes the definition of the term in the middle of the argument.

"You can't say that I'm not being supportive. I still pay you."

Amphiboly: This is a vagueness in grammar that disguises or alters the meaning.

"I heard you already: you said you want me to do it. Okay, okay, okay."

Accent: This changes the meaning of a statement with a changed emphasis on specific words.

"I don't really <u>know</u> what happened."

Misleading vividness: This describes an event (however rare) in vivid detail to make it appear to be larger or more grotesque than it actually is.

"His mistake was so earth-shatteringly significant that it really is a catastrophe."

Argument by verbosity: Multiple levels (legitimate or not) of a situation are raised, creating a complexity of issues that are too extensive to be adequately addressed.

"Your prejudice from some childhood psychosis is driving you to taint

these people's opinions."

False equivalence: This suggests that two concepts are equivalent when they are not.

"The master-slave relationship isn't much different from an employer-employee one."

Reification: This treats a concept or ideal as if it were a reality.

"You can't teach an old dog new tricks, so I'm not going to bother trying."

Straw man: By misrepresenting the opposing position, it is dismissed.

"They have no idea what they are talking about."

Composition: This transfers the attributes of a part to its whole.

"You haven't seen her get angry, but I have. She is a very bitter person."

Division: This transfers the attributes of the whole to one of its specific parts.

"His life is such a mess. He won't be able to find anybody to hire him."

Fallacies of Presumption

Circular reasoning: This secretly assumes what you are trying to prove.

"My behavior should not be questioned, because I know that I am a good person."

Post hoc ergo propter hoc: This improperly assumes that a sequence in time implies a cause and effect.

"You didn't get a good night's sleep and now you start yelling. It's not

about me at all."

Complex question: This is a loaded question crafted so there is no legitimate response.
"Have you always been this impossible?"

False Dilemma: This reduces the choices to two unpleasant extremes, though there are other options.
"You either do it this way or fail. The choice is yours."

Hasty generalization: This assumes a broad conclusion based on a small sample.
"He seems to be such a pleasant man. He can't be as bad as you say."

Cherry picking: This points to specific facts that support its viewpoint, while ignoring the facts that do not.
"My success speaks for itself. That is all you need to know."

Moving the goal post: This dismisses the sound evidence presented to defend an argument and sets up some other (often greater) demand for proof.
"That professional's opinion is just his opinion. You need to prove it with numbers."

Shifting the burden of proof: Rather than bothering to prove his claim true, he requires the opposition to prove it false.
"You have some deep, dark secret, and you're mentally blaming me for it. I'm sure of it."

Continuum fallacy: This rejects a claim entirely because it was not completely precise.
"This is no good. It doesn't deal with the specifics of each case."

Nirvana fallacy: This is when solutions to a problem are rejected because they are not perfect.

"That won't work. It doesn't accomplish all of our ideals."

Argument from silence: This is a conclusion that is based on the absence of a specified type of evidence.

"You haven't found a professional who agrees with you, though."

Misinterpreted silence: This assumes because no counterargument was immediately offered, then there is none.

"Since you offer no reply, I'll assume I'm right."

Argument to moderation: This assumes that the compromise between the two positions is always correct.

"If you take the best of both ideas, you will have something worth doing."

Circular cause and consequence: This claims the consequence of a situation to be its main cause.

"I drink because you don't show me enough respect."

Single cause: This assumes that there is only one, simple cause for an event, when there actually are many significant contributions to it.

"This company is failing, and it is all because you had no vision!"

False conditional: This argues for some action (often not good) to prove the truth of the antecedent.

"If you loved me, you would show it by giving me what I want."

Self Test

Read each scenario and determine which manipulation tactic(s) is being used. Speed actually is the final goal but concentrate on accuracy for this test. You need to be able to identify what is happening enough to respond appropriately, boldly, and quickly.

Assume what has been said or done previously is just, reasonable, and well-presented. How might these statements be used as manipulation?

1. "What do you mean that you don't have a voice? Of course you do. You're talking now, aren't you?"
2. "If you are the Son of God, throw yourself down from here."
3. "You have to expect that I would behave the way I do. I have a great deal of weight on my shoulders. What I am doing is exactly what anyone else would do in my shoes."
4. "What you did has upset her. Look how miserable you are making her. You need to change your decision."
5. "I'm not going to say who, but someone you have always trusted has confided in me that you are behaving completely out of line."
6. "Mr. Hendricks, I want you to meet my star employee [i.e. *you*] here. He can do anything you assign to him (though he will modestly deny it). He's at your disposal for this project. Challenge him."
7. "I'm going to let you handle this. Make sure that [an incredible feat with limited resources gets done impossibly soon]. However you want to arrange doing it is fine."
8. "If you don't help me out, you're going to force me down a dark path. Believe me, you don't want me going there."
9. "If you don't want me to go to your boss and tell him how irresponsible you and your entire team has been in this matter, you need to cooperate with me here."

10. "You didn't tell me how long you wanted me to stay for your meeting, so I scheduled something else. But I will be willing to stay for the fifteen minutes before I have to leave... How horrid of you not to be grateful!"

11. "If you know what you're supposed to do, it shouldn't matter how you feel about doing it—just do it... You haven't given me any good reason why you shouldn't, so I expect you will."

12. "You know what is right in your heart. You're just too afraid to look there."

13. "You can do this for me—we're a team."

14. "Really, I should have as much as you have, yet all you give me is some little token gift. Why *should* I be happy with that?"

15. "How I behave is an expression of who I am. You have to learn to accept me that way."

16. "The past is past. Let bygones be bygones. You can make better choices that will prevent me from getting so upset. We don't want that happening again."

17. "I have been covering for your irresponsibility for years. Here you are trying to dump it on me again! I'm sick of your power plays. You need to take care of the problem yourself; I'm not going to."

18. "I see that you are angry. I'll be praying for you about that."

19. "Nobody believes that you have the moral integrity to do what is right."

20. "Don't be a fool. It's only a problem because you're making it into one."

CPSIA information can be obtained
at www.ICGtesting.com
Printed in the USA
LVHW031349050121
675685LV00026B/675

9 781646 632435